T0331055

Digital Image Processing

This book provides a mix of theoretical and practical perceptions of the related concepts pertaining to image processing. The primary objectives are to offer an overview of the elementary concepts and practices appropriate to digital imaging processing as well as to provide theoretical exposition. The book starts with an expanded coverage of the fundamentals to provide a more comprehensive and cohesive coverage of the topics including but not limited to:

- Applications and tools for image processing, and fundamentals with several implementation examples
- Concepts of image formation
- OpenCV installation with step-by-step screenshots
- Concepts behind intensity, brightness and contrast, and color models
- Ways by which noises are created in an image and the possible remedial measures
- Edge detection, image segmentation, classification, regression, and classification algorithms
- Importance of frequency domain in the image processing field
- Relevant code snippets and the MATLAB® codes, and several interesting sets of simple programs in OpenCV and Python to aid learning and for complete understanding

The video lectures by the authors for specific topics through YouTube enable easy inference for the readers to apply the learned theory into practice. The addition of contents at the end of each chapter such as quizzes and review questions fully prepare readers for further study.

Graduate students, postgraduate students, researchers, and anyone in general interested in image processing, computer vision, machine learning domains, etc. will find this book an excellent starting point for information and an able ally.

Digital Image Processing

A Baskar, Muthaiah Rajappa,
Shriram K Vasudevan,
and T S Murugesh

CRC Press
Taylor & Francis Group
Boca Raton London New York

CRC Press is an imprint of the
Taylor & Francis Group, an **informa** business

A CHAPMAN & HALL BOOK

MATLAB® is a trademark of The MathWorks, Inc. and is used with permission. The MathWorks does not warrant the accuracy of the text or exercises in this book. This book's use or discussion of MATLAB® software or related products does not constitute endorsement or sponsorship by The MathWorks of a particular pedagogical approach or particular use of the MATLAB® software.

First edition published 2023
by CRC Press
6000 Broken Sound Parkway NW, Suite 300, Boca Raton, FL 33487-2742

and by CRC Press
4 Park Square, Milton Park, Abingdon, Oxon, OX14 4RN
CRC Press is an imprint of Taylor & Francis Group, LLC

© 2023: A Baskar, Muthaiah Rajappa, Shriram. K Vasudevan, T S Murugesh

Library of Congress Cataloging-in-Publication Data
Names: Baskar, A., author. | Rajappa, Muthaiah, author. | Vasudevan, Shriram K., author. | Murugesh, T. S., author.
Title: Digital image processing / A. Baskar, Muthaiah Rajappa, Shriram K. Vasudevan, T. S. Murugesh.
Description: First edition. | Boca Raton : Chapman & Hall/CRC Press, [2023] | Includes bibliographical references and index. | Summary: "The book augurs to be a mix of theoretical and practical perceptions of the related concepts pertaining to image processing. The primary objectives orient to offer an overview to the elementary concepts and practices appropriate to DIP as well as to provide theoretical exposition. It starts with an expanded coverage of the fundamentals to provide a more comprehensive and cohesive coverage of the topics"-- Provided by publisher.
Identifiers: LCCN 2022052363 (print) | LCCN 2022052364 (ebook) | ISBN 9781032108575 (hbk) | ISBN 9781032478678 (pbk) | ISBN 9781003217428 (ebk)
Subjects: LCSH: Image processing--Digital techniques.
Classification: LCC TA1637 .P374 2023 (print) | LCC TA1637 (ebook) | DDC 006.4/2--dc23/eng/20221110
LC record available at https://lccn.loc.gov/2022052363
LC ebook record available at https://lccn.loc.gov/2022052364

ISBN: 9781032108575 (hbk)
ISBN: 9781032478678 (pbk)
ISBN: 9781003217428 (ebk)

DOI: 10.1201/9781003217428

Typeset in Palatino
by Deanta Global Publishing Services, Chennai, India

Contents

Preface...ix
Authors xi

1 Introduction to Image Processing: Fundamentals First 1
Learning Objectives...1
1.1 Introduction 1
1.2 What Is an Image?...2
1.3 What Is Image Processing? 2
1.4 What is a Pixel?...3
1.5 Types of Images..4
1.6 Applications of Image Processing 8
1.7 Tools for Image Processing 11
      1.7.1   OpenCV for Windows: Installation Procedure 12
1.8 Prerequisites to Learn Image Processing 19
1.9 Quiz..19
      1.9.1   Answers..20
1.10 Review Questions 20
      1.10.1 Answers..21
Further Reading 22

2 Image Processing Fundamentals...23
Learning Objectives...23
2.1 Introduction 23
2.2 Concept of Image Formation...24
2.3 Bits per Pixel 29
2.4 Intensity, Brightness, and Contrast: Must-Know Concepts 30
2.5 Pixel Resolution and Pixel Density..31
2.6 Understanding the Color Models 34
      2.6.1   What Is a Color Model?...34
      2.6.2   RGB Color Model and CMY Color Model...........................34
      2.6.3   HSV Color Model..36
      2.6.4   YUV Color Model 37
2.7 Characteristics of Image Operations..44
      2.7.1   Types of Operations...44
      2.7.2   Types of Neighborhoods...45
2.8 Different Types of Image Formats...46
      2.8.1   TIFF (Tag Image File Format) 47
      2.8.2   JPEG (Joint Photographic Experts Group)........................47
      2.8.3   GIF (Graphics Interchange Format).....................................48

2.8.4   PNG (Portable Network Graphic) 49
2.8.5   RAW Format 49
2.9   Steps in Digital Image Processing 49
2.10   Elements of Digital Image Processing System 51
2.11   Quiz 53
       2.11.1 Answers 54
2.12   Review Questions 54
       2.12.1 Answers 55
Further Reading 58

3 **Image Noise: A Clear Understanding** 61
Learning Objectives 61
3.1   Introduction 61
3.2   Photoelectronic Noise 63
       3.2.1   Photon Noise (Also Called Shot Noise or
               Poisson Noise) 63
       3.2.2   Thermal Noise 64
       3.2.3   How to Overcome Photoelectronic Noise?
               (Thermal Noise/Photon Noise) 64
3.3   Impulse Noise 65
       3.3.1   Salt-and-Pepper Noise 66
       3.3.2   How to Overcome Impulse Noise? 66
3.4   Structured Noise 67
3.5   Quiz 69
       3.5.1   Answers 69
3.6   Review Questions 69
       3.6.1   Answers 70
Further Reading 70

4 **Edge Detection: From a Clear Perspective** 73
Learning Objectives 73
4.1   Introduction 73
4.2   Why Detect Edges? 74
4.3   Modeling Intensity Changes/Types of Edges: A Quick Lesson .. 74
4.4   Steps in Edge Detection 77
4.5   Sobel Operator 79
4.6   Prewitt Edge Detector 83
4.7   Robinson Edge Detector 86
4.8   Krisch Edge Detector 88
4.9   Canny Edge Detection 91
4.10   Laplacian: The Second-Order Derivatives 100
4.11   Review Questions 104
       4.11.1 Answers 104
Further Reading 105

5 Frequency Domain Processing 107
Learning Objectives 107
5.1   Introduction 107
5.2   Frequency Domain Flow 109
5.3   Low-Pass Filters: A Deeper Dive 110
       5.3.1   Ideal Low-Pass Filter 110
       5.3.2   Butterworth Low-Pass Filter 113
       5.3.3   Gaussian Low-Pass Filter 115
5.4   High-Pass Filters/Sharpening Filters 119
       5.4.1   Ideal High-Pass Filter 119
       5.4.2   Butterworth High-Pass Filter 121
       5.4.3   Gaussian High-Pass Filter 123
5.5   Quiz 127
       5.5.1   Answers 128
5.6   Review Questions 128
       5.6.1   Answers 128
Further Reading 129

6 Image Segmentation: A Clear Analysis and Understanding 131
Learning Objectives 131
6.1   Introduction 131
6.2   Types of Segmentation 134
6.3   Thresholding Method 136
       6.3.1   Segmentation Algorithm Based on a Global
                Threshold 136
       6.3.2   Segmentation Algorithm Based on Multiple
                Thresholds 142
6.4   Histogram-Based Segmentation 142
       6.4.1   Segmentation Algorithm Based on a Variable
                Threshold 143
       6.4.2   Variable Thresholding through Image Partitioning 144
6.5   Region-Based Segmentation 145
       6.5.1   Region-Growing Method 145
       6.5.2   Region Split-and-Merge Technique 147
6.6   Edge-Based Segmentation 150
6.7   Clustering-Based Segmentation 150
6.8   Morphological Transforms-Based Segmentation 150
       6.8.1   Dilation and Erosion 151
       6.8.2   Opening and Closing 158
       6.8.3   Hit-or-Miss Transform 159
6.9   Review Questions 160
       6.9.1   Answers 161
Further Reading 162

7 Classification: A Must-Know Concept 163
      Learning Objectives 163
      7.1   Introduction 163
      7.2   Support Vector Machine (SVM) 164
              7.2.1   Hyperplane 164
              7.2.2   Support Vectors 165
              7.2.3   Margin 165
      7.3   How SVMs Work? 165
      7.4   k-Nearest Neighbor (k-NN) 166
      7.5   Clustering: An Interesting Concept to Know 170
              7.5.1   k-Means Clustering 170
      7.6   Quiz 175
      Further Reading 175

8 Playing with OpenCV and Python 177
      8.1   Introduction 177
      8.2   Ubuntu and OpenCV Installation 177
      8.3   Image Resizing 179
      8.4   Image Blurring 180
      8.5   Image Borders 182
      8.6   Image Conversion to Grayscale Format with OpenCV 183
      8.7   Edge Detection with OpenCV 183
      8.8   Counting Objects with OpenCV 185
      8.9   Predicting Forest Fire with OpenCV 185

Index 191

Preface

Image processing, a rapidly growing technology, is a type of signal processing where some operations are performed on an image, so as to obtain an enhanced image or to extract some valuable information from it.

Digital image processing (DIP) is a constantly evolving field with new algorithms and techniques and is certainly worth learning if one is interested in image processing, computer vision, machine learning, etc. Learners who wish to get started with image processing can find this book an able ally to learn DIP from scratch. The popularity of DIP includes many reasons starting from enhancing the quality of digital images, image restoration techniques, removing noise from digital images, and compressing digital images thereby conserving memory space be it on a computer or storage device. The primary objectives of this book orient to offer an overview to the elementary concepts and practices appropriate to DIP as well as to provide theoretical exposition.

This book starts with an expanded coverage of the fundamentals, image types, applications, and tools for image processing. Later, the vistas are extended to the concepts of image formation, unraveling the concepts behind intensity, brightness and contrast, and color models, and details the steps in DIP as well as its components. The following chapter deals with noise in an image and types of image noise, addresses the ways by which noise is created in an image, and deals with the possible remedial measures.

The subsequent chapters deal with edge detection and its operators followed by frequency domain processing, which, along with all the MATLAB codes, provide more comprehensive and cohesive coverage of the topics under purview. This book then moves toward image segmentation to deliver a clear analysis and for a thorough understanding, and then introduces the must-know concepts of classification and regression and also explains the concepts of a few frequently used classification algorithms. Finally, the readers are presented with several interesting sets of simple programs in OpenCV and Python to help enhance their understanding. Also, the same has been presented as video lectures through YouTube by the authors to enable the readers to apply the theory they have learned into practice. The addition of content at the end of each chapter such as quizzes and review questions fully prepare readers for further study.

Authors

A Baskar is a seasoned academician with close to two decades of experience in teaching and research. He is currently associated with the Department of Computer Science and Engineering, Amrita School of Computing, Amrita Vishwa Vidyapeetham, Coimbatore, India. He is an expert in the areas of image and video processing, Internet of Things, and computer vision. Baskar has guided over 15 master's projects and many undergraduate projects. Baskar also has many published articles with refereed international journals. He has presented papers at international and national conferences. He is also associated with boards of studies in many colleges of high repute. He has also won awards from the likes of Infosys and Accenture for his teaching and research skills.

Muthaiah Rajappa is a professor and associate dean in information technology and information communication technology at the School of Computing, Shanmugha Arts, Science, Technology & Research Academy (SASTRA) (deemed-to-be-university), Thanjavur, India. He obtained his bachelor's degree in electronics and instrumentation engineering from Annamalai University, Tamil Nadu, India, in 1989. He completed his master's degree in power electronics from Shanmuga College of Engineering, Tamil Nadu, India, in 1997. He was awarded a doctorate in the area of image compression by SASTRA in 2008. Rajappa has published more than 100 research articles in many reputed journals. He also has contributed through paper publications, and review and chairing sessions in many conferences. He has completed multiple funded projects from organizations of high repute and national importance.

Shriram K Vasudevan obtained his bachelor's degree in electronics and instrumentation from Annamalai University, Tamil Nadu, in 2004, master's degree in embedded systems from the Shanmugha Arts, Science, Technology & Research Academy (deemed-to-be-university), Thanjavur, India, in 2007, and doctorate in embedded systems from Ponnaiyah Ramajayam Institute of Science and Technology (PRIST) University, Tamil Nadu, India, in 2015. He earned his master of business administration degree in human resource management and marketing from Periyar Maniammai University, Tamil Nadu, India, in 2008. Over the course of 16 years, he has obtained a blend of industrial and teaching experience. He has authored/coauthored 45 books for reputed publishers across the globe. He has authored 140 research papers in revered international journals and 30 papers in international/national conferences. He is currently associated with Intel, India. Prior, he was associated with Wipro Technologies, VIT University, Aricent Technologies, Amrita University, and L&T Technology Services. He holds the Corporate Fellow Membership in IETE and is an ACM Distinguished Speaker, CSI

Distinguished Speaker, NASSCOM Prime Ambassador, NVIDIA DLI, and Intel Software Innovator. He has a YouTube channel bearing his name through which he teaches thousands of people all around the world. He has been recognized/honored for his technical expertise by Factana, Accumulate, Telecommunications and the Digital Government Regulatory Authority (United Arab Emirates), ZyBooks (Wiley Brand), AOTMP, Adani Digital, NASSCOM Foundation, World Summit on the Information Society (WSIS), De-Nora, IIT Kharagpur E Cell, Huawei, NVIDIA, Cubestop, IETE, Datastax, Honda, Wiley, AGBI, ACM, Uletkz, *The Hindu* (Tamil), Exact Sciences Corp, Proctor and Gamble Innovation Centre (India), Dinamalar, AWS (Amazon Web Services), Sabre Technologies, IEEE Compute, Syndicate Bank, MHRD, Elsevier, Bounce, IncubateInd, Smart India Hackathon, Stop the Bleed, HackHarvard (Harvard University), Accenture Digital (India), NEC (Nippon Electric Company, Japan), Thought Factory (Axis Bank Innovation Lab), Rakuten (Japan), Titan, Future Group, Institution of Engineers of India (IEI), Ministry of Food Processing Industries (MoFPI – Government of India), Intel, Microsoft, Wipro, Infosys, IBM India, SoS Ventures (USA), VIT University, Amrita University, Computer Society of India, TBI–TIDE, ICTACT, *Times of India*, Nehru Group of Institutions, Texas Instruments, IBC Cambridge, Cisco, CII (Confederation of Indian Industries), Indian Air Force, DPSRU Innovation & Incubation Foundation, and EL Equipments (Coimbatore). He is a certified Scrum Master. He is also listed in many famous biographical databases. He has delivered talks at various international conferences and forums of high repute. Vasudevan has also been granted many patents. He is a hackathon enthusiast and has won about 50 hackathons, including HackHarvard 2019.

T S Murugesh obtained his bachelor's degree in electronics and instrumentation in 1999, master's degree in process control and instrumentation in 2005, and doctorate in instrumentation engineering in 2015, all from Annamalai University, Tamil Nadu, India. He possesses a vast experience of nearly 23 years in academia in the field of analog and digital electronics, automation and control, IoT, system design, instrumentation, image processing, and computational bioengineering. After a tenure of almost 19 years with the Department of Electronics and Instrumentation Engineering, belonging to the Faculty of Engineering and Technology, Annamalai University, he is currently an associate professor in the Department of Electronics and Communication Engineering, Government College of Engineering Srirangam, Tiruchirappalli, Tamil Nadu, India.

He has delivered four talks at international conferences of high repute such as the 3rd Edition of International Conference on Materials Science and Engineering (MAT 2022) organized by Magnus Group LLC, Chicago, Illinois, as well as at the 5th Virtual Congress on Materials Science and Engineering, "Materials Info 2022" organized by Mind Authors, Inc., Beaverton, Oregon. He has delivered invited lectures at the national level in various institutions including Sastra University, Annamalai University, Manakula Vinayagar

Institute of Technology – Puducherry, Government College of Engineering Srirangam, Madurai Institute of Engineering and Technology, and P.A. College of Engineering and Technology – Pollachi and Viswajyothi College of Engineering and Technology, Kerala. He has delivered invited lectures in faculty development programs organized by the Faculty Training Centre, Government College of Technology, Coimbatore, in association with the Government College of Engineering – Thanjavur, and another one with Government College of Engineering – Salem, and also in a national-level webinar conducted on behalf of "Unnat Bharat Abhiyan", a flagship program of the Ministry of Education, Government of India.

To his credit, he has around three dozen peer-reviewed indexed publications including Springer Nature, Elsevier, and Inderscience; has organized a one-week AICTE Training And Learning (ATAL) Academy-sponsored FDP; conducted a few workshops at the national level; and is a reviewer for IEEE, Inderscience, and a few other peer-reviewed journals. He has acted as a primary evaluator for the Government of India's Smart India Hackathon 2022 (Software & Hardware Edition) as well as Toycathon 2021 and also as a judge in the grand finale for the Government of India's Toycathon 2021, an inter-ministerial initiative organized by the Ministry of Education's Innovation Cell with support from AICTE (All India Council for Technical Education). He is an AICTE and NITTTR-certified mentor under the National Initiative for Technical Teachers Training and also a Certified Microsoft Educator Academy Professional. He is also a reviewer of B.E / B.Tech Technical Books in Regional Language scheme of AICTE coordinated by the Centre for Development of Tamil in Engineering and Technology, Anna University, Tamil Nadu, India. He is a Master Assessor for the prestigious Naan Mudhalvan Program devised by the Government of Tamil Nadu. He was appreciated by Huawei for his academic collaboration and was issued a Huawei developers certification. Murugesh mentored the team that won first prize for the problem statement "Employment tracking and traceability system – Organized sector", given by the Ministry of Labour Employment, Government of India, during the grand finale of Smart India Hackathon 2022 Software Edition. He is a hackathon enthusiast and his team has won the FIRST Prize in the 2022, Cloud Fest Hackathon 2 presented by Google Cloud as well as in the DigitalGov Hack, the Hackathon by WSIS Forum 2023 and Digital Government Authority, Saudi Arabia and also bagged the second Prize in the IFG x TA Hub Hackathon 2022. He is a conference committee member as well as a publishing committee member for the International Association of Applied Science and Technology. He also holds the editorial board membership of American Journal of Embedded Systems and Applications. He has authored two books for CRC Press/Taylor & Francis Group (UK) and is authoring a book for Nova Science Publishers, Inc. (USA) and 2 more books for CRC Press. He is a professional body member of the Institution of Engineers (India).

1

Introduction to Image Processing: Fundamentals First

Learning Objectives

After reading this chapter, the reader should have a clear understanding about:

- What an image is all about?
- Why an image is processed?
- What makes an image?
- Potential applications of image processing
- Prerequisites for deeper learning
- Tools available for image processing

1.1 Introduction

There is a general saying: "A picture is worth a thousand words". In this book we are going to learn out-and-out about images. Image processing is one of the evergreen fields of computer science and engineering. It keeps evolving, and researchers are consistently working on developing image processing techniques that provide more features and better accuracy with increased speed. A special mention goes to the high-speed processing engines that are available and affordable nowadays. Also, image storage has become much cheaper. The following discussion should enable the reader to understand what an image is, what can be understood from an image, how much information can be retrieved from an image, and what sort of applications can be developed from the available information. Stay tuned! Fun awaits you!

DOI: 10.1201/9781003217428-1

1.2 What Is an Image?

Before dwelling deeper, it is important to understand the fundamentals. Being strong in the fundamentals will help you throughout this learning journey.

Disclaimer: We have titled the book "digital image processing". Hence, we shall deal with digital images.

According to dictionary definitions, an image, be it digital or still, is only a binary representation of some visual information. The visual information can be a simple drawing, photograph, recorded graphs, organization logos, or anything of this sort. All these images have something in common. If they are digital images, they all can be stored and saved for future use electronically on any storage device. Figure 1.1 presents a sample image with information inside it. This image is a traffic sign, which gives information about the signals and signage for drivers. This is a digital image and can be stored in any digital storage medium. To be more precise, this image was shot with a digital camera.

1.3 What Is Image Processing?

Assume someone sees the signage in Figure 1.1 on a road. Immediately, their eyes will start capturing the content, and the brain interprets what the signals signify. Based on the understanding, one would move farther. In digital image processing, the same image can be fed as input into the system, and

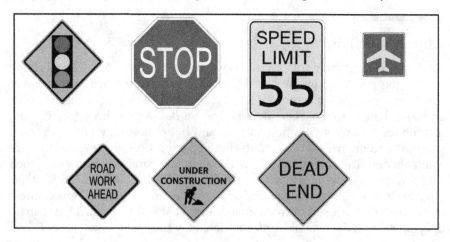

FIGURE 1.1
The first image – image with information – digital Image.

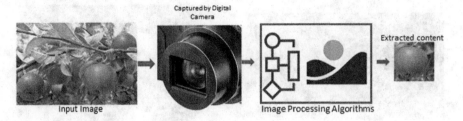

FIGURE 1.2
The "image" processing.

the system would interpret and understand the content to let further actions happen. The algorithms developed play a major role in understanding the content with higher accuracy.

Image processing helps users understand the content and context from any image. Appropriate processing techniques are to be chosen to get the best results.

> *To summarize*: Image processing enables us to perform the required operations on a particular image that could help in either enhancing the image or extracting information from the image. Image processing can be categorized as one of the fields of signal processing. For an image processing system, like any other system, there should be input (an image) and output as well. The output enhances the image or features/characteristics from the image, which help in precisely identifying the contents.

Being this is an image processing book, it is always a good idea to represent any concept through an image. Refer to Figure 1.2 that presents the image processing concept in a nutshell.

1.4 What is a Pixel?

One should understand that an image is nothing but an array or a matrix of multiple pixels properly arranged in columns and rows. Now, it is also good to understand what a pixel is. The word *pixel* originates from "picture element". A pixel is the smallest unit in a digital image. Multiple pixels arranged in rows and columns form an image. An image is fully composed of pixels. Figure 1.3 has a picture on the left-hand side (LHS) and the right-hand side (RHS); the pixels from a particular region of the image can be seen. This will help you understand that multiple pixels are arranged appropriately to get

FIGURE 1.3
Pixels.

a meaningful digital image. The LHS is a complete image, whereas the RHS represents a part of the same but in the form of pixels. The boxes highlighted on the RHS image represent the individual pixels. Such multiple individual pixels are there in the real image. To make it concise, pixels are the smallest units that form an image. Many more technical details on pixels are presented in Chapter 2.

1.5 Types of Images

The next very important area of discussion is the types of images. They are as follows:

1. Binary image.

   As one could have guessed, binary is all about 0s and 1s. A binary will contain only two colors: white and black. Black is represented by 0 and white is represented by 1. Each pixel in this type of image will have either a value of 0 or 1, representing black or white, respectively (Figure 1.4). In the binary image, each pixel needs only 1 bit of storage space. Be it white or black, what we need is just 1 bit to store that pixel. This is an important aspect to be remembered and this will help in distinguishing the binary image from the black-and-white image.

2. Black-and-white image.

   Most beginners are confused about what a binary image is and what a black-and-white image is. There is a very fundamental difference that differentiates the two. When it comes to black-and-white images, each pixel needs 8 bits of storage space. Each of these pixels can have a 0 or 1. Again, 0 represents black and 1 represents white. Multiple 0s and 1s are in an image, but the storage requirement for the pixels is much higher. This gives smoothness and enriched quality to the image (Figure 1.5).

FIGURE 1.4
A binary image.

FIGURE 1.5
A typical black-and-white image.

3. Grayscale image.

   The next type of image to be discussed is the grayscale image. It is a special image that has a range of shades from black to white, i.e., the shades should be between white and black. Often people regard this as no color and they refer to the shades of white and black. The most commonly used format is the 8-bit format and it accommodates

256 different shades. The range of these shades is from 0 (black) to 255 (white) and in-between are the different shades. Figure 1.6 presents the grayscale shading pattern. A sample grayscale image is presented in Figure 1.7.

4. Color image.

Each pixel in a color image has color information. Each pixel in a color image is composed of three channels, and they are most commonly regarded as R, G, and B, representing the colors red, green, and blue, respectively. In this type of image, one should again visualize the image as a matrix. Each box (pixel) in the matrix is composed of three components: R, G, and B channels. Each of these channels needs 8 bits for storage, hence each pixel is 24 bits. Hence, it should be understood that R, G, and B together constitute a pixel in a color image. The shade of each of the pixels vary based on the intensity of R or G or B. Each of these R or G or B channels individually has 256 shades in it. With all these shades we could produce a beautiful color image with all good colors captured.

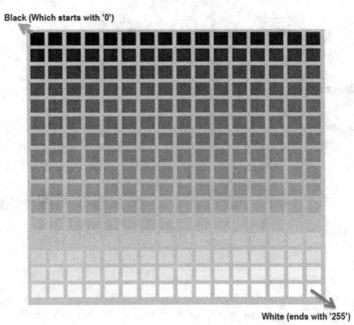

Note:
All the boxes in the matrix represent the transition that happened from black to white.

Black (Which starts with '0')

White (ends with '255')

FIGURE 1.6
Grayscale shading pattern.

FIGURE 1.7
A sample grayscale image.

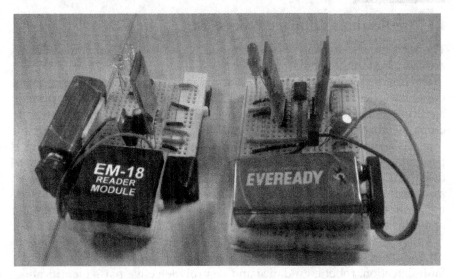

FIGURE 1.8
Sample input image.

A sample image has been taken, as shown in Figure 1.8. R, G, and B have been extracted. This should help readers understand that R, G, and B constitute a color image. Also, in Figure 1.9, the intensity of R, G, and B are presented individually.

The types of images have been explained. The next topic to be discussed is the applications of image processing and it should provide a detailed view of where this learning is helpful.

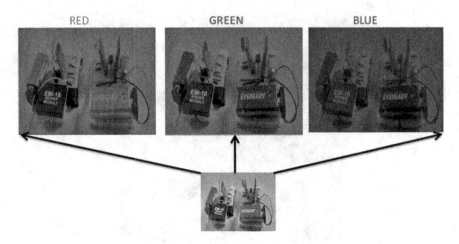

FIGURE 1.9
RGB composition.

1.6 Applications of Image Processing

The applications of image processing are wide-ranging and some of them are described in the following.

The first sector where image processing has enormous application potential is in agriculture. Image processing techniques can be used to develop applications for sorting fruits, grading fruit quality, identifying disease in crops, locating weeds, and identifying species, for example (Figure 1.10).

In the automobile sector, image processing has many applications and is particularly used in critical safety applications. Applications include lane detection, license plate detection, toll collection systems, accident impact assessment, driver assistance systems, and rear and front cameras for parking applications. Many researchers are actively working toward building safer and smarter image processing–based automobile applications (Figure 1.11).

As far as industry is concerned, image processing has numerous applications. They include quality control applications, inspection applications, fault detection, robotic guidance and control, defective parts identification, and color identification. Machine vision is a boom that is completely based on image processing. Figure 1.12 shows common applications of image processing in industry.

Image processing has found some fantastic applications in the medical field. Image processing can be used for diagnostic purposes. X-ray or scan images can be read and understood to see the variations or symptoms of many diseases. Recent developments have ensured that robots can perform surgeries, of which image processing is a very important component. Cancer cell detection, tumor detection, and stent placement are other major areas where image processing is highly useful (Figure 1.13).

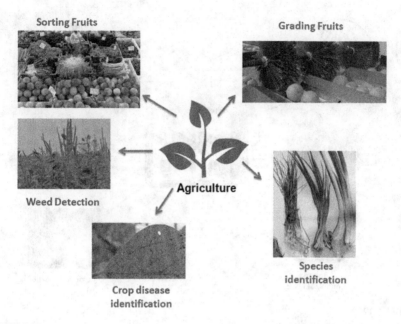

FIGURE 1.10
Image processing and agriculture.

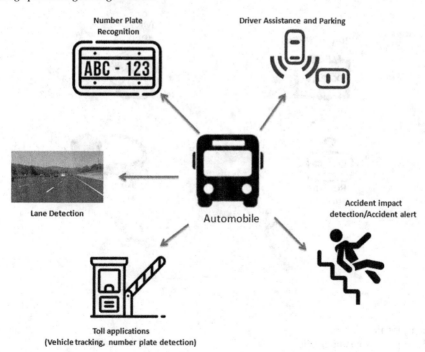

FIGURE 1.11
Image processing and automobiles.

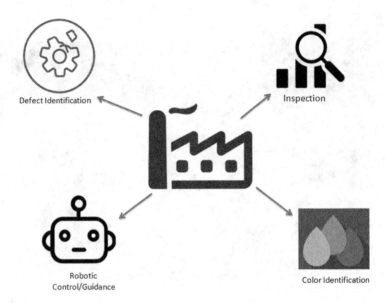

FIGURE 1.12
Image processing and industry.

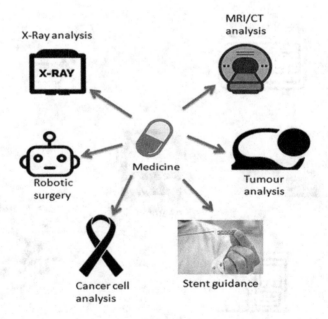

FIGURE 1.13
Image processing and medicine.

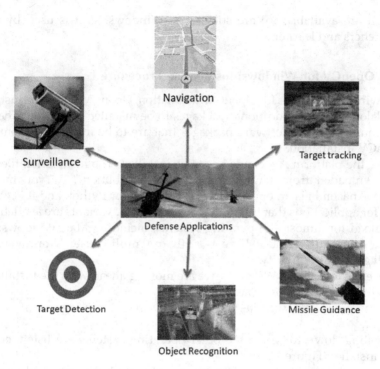

FIGURE 1.14
Image processing and defense.

Image processing has vast applications in the defense industry and is frequently employed in defense and security-related applications. A few applications include target detection and target tracking, missile guidance, navigation, surveillance, and object recognition. Also, during a war or crisis, drones, which have image processing techniques embedded within their cameras, are used for recovery operations (Figure 1.14).

Having learned the applications one can have for image processing, it is time to learn the tools and support available for implementing and building image processing–based systems.

1.7 Tools for Image Processing

Three of the most prominent tools one should use/learn to work on image processing are MATLAB, OpenCV, and Python.

Since MATLAB installation is not a challenging task, we have focused on providing the guidelines for OpenCV installation. Also, installation of Python is provided. Though the Ubuntu variant of both the OpenCV and

Python are available, we are sticking to Windows, as it is used by most researchers and learners.

1.7.1 OpenCV for Windows: Installation Procedure

Following are the steps for OpenCV installation. OpenCV cannot be installed standalone; it needs additional packages to be installed alongside. The section enumerates the software packages that are to be installed to complete OpenCV installation.

First, the platform Anaconda has to be installed. The installation files can be downloaded from www.anaconda.com/distribution/. As you may be aware, Anaconda is an open-source distribution for Python and it is widely used for applications that involve voluminous data. Variants are available for download for almost all operating systems, including Mac, Windows, and Linux. Anaconda is said to have more than 10 million users worldwide and is still gaining popularity.

Since the focus is on Windows, we are moving ahead with the installation guidelines for a Windows-based machine.

Upon opening the website, the following screen, as in Figure 1.15, should appear.

Scrolling down to where the other operating systems are listed, choose your installer (Figure 1.16).

After clicking the download button, as in Figure 1.15, users are directed to the screen as shown in Figure 1.17, upon which the Python 3.9 version, 64-Bit Graphical Installer (594 MB) is downloaded.

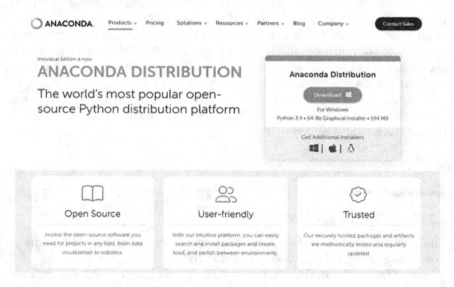

FIGURE 1.15
Welcome screen of Anaconda site.

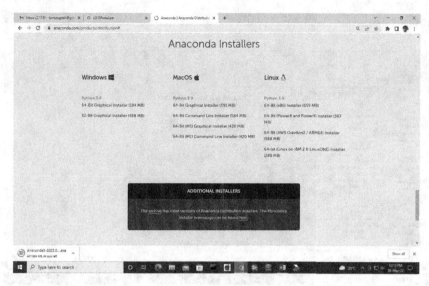

FIGURE 1.16
Anaconda installers.

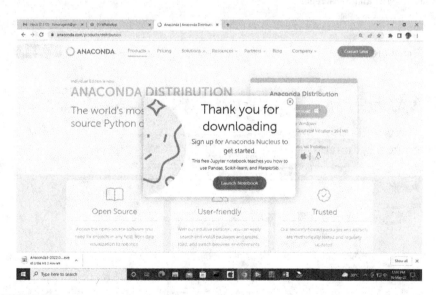

FIGURE 1.17
Python version.

The installation can be started once the download is complete. Once the extraction is done from the executable files, the screen in Figure 1.18 should be visible.

Agree to the license requirements (Figure 1.19), then proceed to the next step.

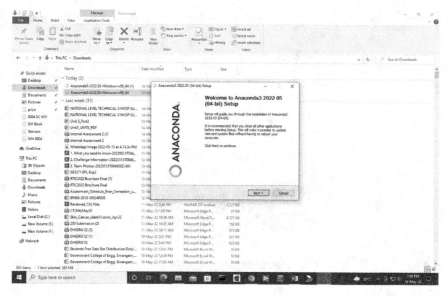

FIGURE 1.18
Anaconda installation screen.

FIGURE 1.19
License agreement.

The user is prompted to select the mode of availability of Anaconda: for everyone or just the user who has logged in. Select the appropriate choice (see Figure 1.20).

Next, select the destination folder; 3 GB of space is required. Hence, choose the folder wisely (Figure 1.21).

The next screen presents the advanced installation options (Figure 1.22). It is best to go with both options presented.

Once done, click install and installation continues. One can follow the progress, as shown in Figure 1.23. This process should take time.

Once done, a screen with a message as shown in Figure 1.24 appears.

Once this is done, we are all set to go! The content in Figure 1.25 will be displayed if installation has gone well.

That's it. Anaconda is installed. But, the game is not yet over.

One should test whether the installation has been done properly. For that, go to the command prompt. Typing "cmd" should bring up the command prompt. In that command window, type the command "python". The confirmation of correct installation is shown (Figure 1.26).

Upon successful installation of Python, it is important to install OpenCV with the command "pip install opencv-python" in the Anaconda prompt (Figure 1.27).

One can also validate if the OpenCV has been installed successfully, through the sequence in the command prompt in Figure 1.28.

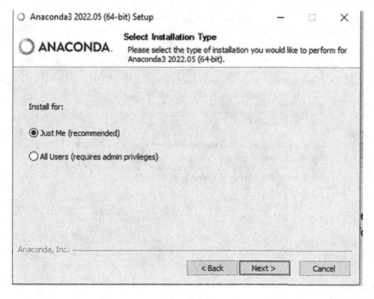

FIGURE 1.20
Installation options.

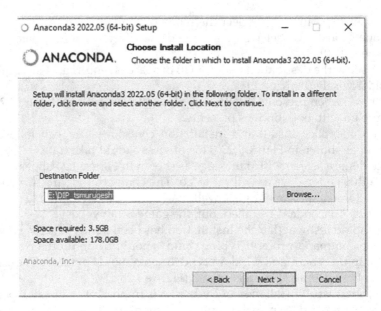

FIGURE 1.21
Installation directory.

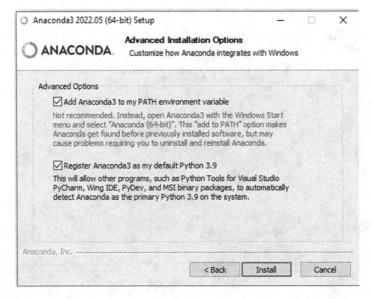

FIGURE 1.22
Advanced installation options.

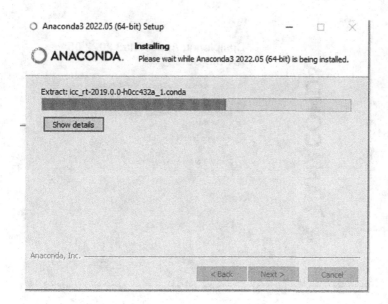

FIGURE 1.23
The progress.

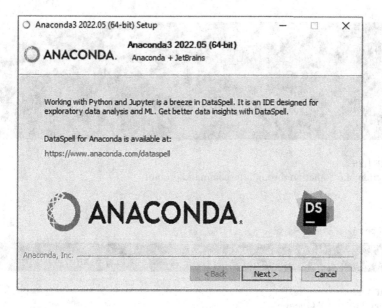

FIGURE 1.24
Anaconda DataSpell IDE.

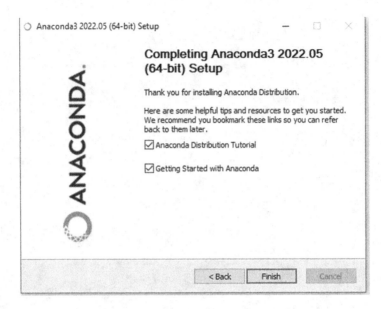

FIGURE 1.25
Anaconda installation complete.

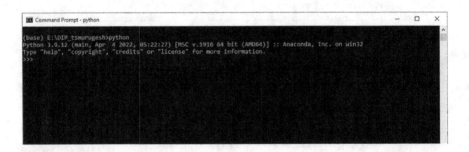

FIGURE 1.26
Verification of installation through the command prompt.

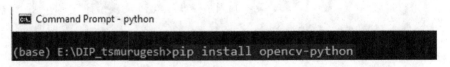

FIGURE 1.27
Command to install OpenCV.

```
(base) C:\Users\shrir>python
Python 3.9.12 (main, Apr  4 2022, 05:22:27) [MSC v.1916 64 bit (AMD64)] :: Anaconda, Inc. on win32
Type "help", "copyright", "credits" or "license" for more information.
>>> import cv2
>>> cv2.__version__
'4.6.0'
>>> _
```

FIGURE 1.28
Confirmation of successful OpenCV installation.

1.8 Prerequisites to Learn Image Processing

The fundamental prerequisite to learning more about image processing is interest. Following is a list of desirable learner qualities to make the learning process faster and better.

An image is represented using math, thus the subject can't be ignored. Fundamental know-how of the following is beneficial:

1. Linear algebra
2. Probability and statistics
3. Signals and systems
4. Differential equations
5. Digital electronics
6. Programming skills (or the logic)

Do not be intimidated by the list! We will make sure the learning is imparted in the way that is practical.

It is hoped that this chapter refreshed your must-know fundamentals of image processing. It's time to move on to learning the basic concepts of image formation, characteristics of image operations, and image types in the next chapter.

1.9 Quiz

1. Every image has some information inside. True or false?
2. All images must be even sized. True or false?
3. Image processing is all about understanding the _____ and _____ of an image.
4. Image processing techniques are meant to only understand the image. True or false?

5. A _____ is the fundamental component of an image.

6. An image is fully composed of multiple _____.

7. The binary image is a combination of _____ and _____.

8. The size of each pixel in a binary image is _____.

9. A black-and-white image is a combination of _____ and _____.

10. The size of the black-and-white pixel in a black-and-white image is _____.

11. A grayscale image is a combination of _____.

12. A color image has _____, _____, and _____ pixels.

1.9.1 Answers

1. True

2. False

3. Context and content

4. False. It can be used to enhance the image.

5. Pixel

6. Pixels.

7. 0s and 1s (representing black and white)

8. One bit.

9. Black and white (0s and 1s).

10. 8 bits

11. Range of colors between black and white

12. Red, green, and blue

1.10 Review Questions

1. Define image.

2. Define image processing.

3. Why process an image?

4. What is a pixel and how is it important for an image?

5. What are the types of images you know?

6. Are the black-and-white and grayscale images the same in terms of the content? Explain.

7. How is a binary image different from a black-and-white image?

8. Explain the way color images are constructed.

9. List the storage requirements for all the image types.

10. Name some sectors that use image processing applications.

1.10.1 Answers

1. An image, be it digital or still, is a binary representation of some visual information. The visual information can be a simple drawing, photograph, recorded graphs, organization logos, or anything of this sort.

2. Image processing enables us to perform the required operations on a particular image, which could help in either enhancing the image or extracting information from the image. One can categorize image processing as one of the fields of signal processing. Like any other system, for an image processing system there should be input (an image), and there will be output as well. The output will enhance the image or features/characteristics of the image, which should help in precisely identifying the contents.

3. Image processing helps users in understanding the content and context from any image. Appropriate processing techniques are to be chosen to get the best results.

4. One should understand that an image is nothing but an array or a matrix of multiple pixels that are properly arranged in columns and rows. Now, it is also good to understand what a pixel is. *Pixel* is a word formed from "picture element". A pixel is the smallest unit in a digital image. Multiple pixels arranged in rows and columns actually form an image. An image is fully composed of pixels.

5. Binary, black and white, grayscale, and color.

6. No. Both are different. Black-and-white images are composed of only black or white. But, grayscale is a combination of different shades of black or white (256 shades).

7. Binary image needs 1 bit per pixel storage and the pixel is either black or white. But, a black-and-white image needs 8 bits per pixel for storage. Black-and-white images will be dense and render better quality.

8. Each pixel in the color image has color information. Each pixel in the color image is composed of three channels and they are most commonly regarded as R, G, and B, which represent red, green, and blue colors, respectively. In this type of image, one should again visualize the image as a matrix to gain better understanding. Each box (pixel) in the matrix is composed of three components: R, G, and B channels. Each of these channels needs 8 bits for storage, hence, 24

bits for each pixel. It should be understood that R, G, and B together constitute a pixel in a color image.

9. Binary – 1 bit per pixel.

   Black and white – 8 bits per pixel.

   Grayscale – 8 bits per pixel.

   Color – 24 bits per pixel (R, G, and B channels together).

10. Many sectors use image processing applications, including defense, agriculture, medicine, education, space science, and industrial applications.

Further Reading

Abràmoff, M.D., Magalhães, P.J. and Ram, S.J., 2004. Image processing with ImageJ. *Biophotonics International*, 11(7), pp. 36–42.

Jain, A.K., 1989. *Fundamentals of digital image processing.* Englewood Cliffs, NJ: Prentice Hall.

Petrou, M. and Petrou, C., 2010. *Image processing: The fundamentals.* John Wiley & Sons.

Russ, J.C., 2016. *The image processing handbook.* CRC Press.

Sonka, M., Hlavac, V. and Boyle, R., 2014. *Image processing, analysis, and machine vision.* Cengage Learning.

Weeks, A.R., 1996. *Fundamentals of electronic image processing* (pp. 316–414). Bellingham: SPIE Optical Engineering Press.

Young, I.T., Gerbrands, J.J. and Van Vliet, L.J., 1998. *Fundamentals of image processing* (Vol. 841). Delft: Delft University of Technology.

2

Image Processing Fundamentals

DOI: 10.1201/9781003217428-2

Learning Objectives

After reading this chapter, the reader should have a clear understanding about:

- Image formation
- Concept of bits per pixel
- Brightness, contrast, and intensity
- Pixel resolution and pixel density
- Color models
- Characteristics of image operations
- Types of images
- Steps in digital image processing
- Elements of digital image processing

2.1 Introduction

The previous chapter just hinted at information about pixels and the type of images at a very elementary level and may not be sufficient for an aspiring image processing enthusiast. However, this chapter will enhance understanding of the fundamentals of image processing. This chapter provides clear-cut information about pixels, including more technical details. Also, this chapter dives deeper with some implementation examples for the concepts being dealt with. This chapter is a mix of theoretical and practical understanding of the concepts. Again, it is very important for the reader to have installed the software packages detailed in Chapter 1. This chapter concludes with analyzing color models followed by the complete analysis of the steps involved in digital image processing.

2.2 Concept of Image Formation

As discussed earlier, pixels are the very fundamental and basic unit in any image. But the concept has many technicalities embedded in it and is a must-know for any aspirant who loves to work with image processing. This chapter is meant to give more clarity, and it starts with image formation and will navigate to pixels.

It is helpful to compare human eyes with cameras. Both work on the same principles, and in fact the eyes are indeed better. Eyes are the motivation for scientists to invent and improve cameras to capture images. For example, in image processing, the PC or a microcontroller is the central processing unit, whereas for human eyes, it is the brain. The fundamental principle behind the functioning of human eyes and cameras is reflection. Here, physics comes into play. When a light ray falls on any object, the basic tendency is to reflect it back. We should realize that eyes have a lens as well, just like a camera (Figure 2.1), which enables eyes to see the object of focus.

Let's get somewhat technical now. As a first step, it is important to understand the image formation process. This involves a bit of physics as well. Hence, if you have some physics knowledge, it would really be helpful. Have a close look at Figure 2.2. The image formation process is explained in a diagrammatical way for clear understanding. Assume that the camera focuses on the tree with fruits as shown in the figure.

The process of image formation essentially involves the conversion of a 3D scene to a 2D image. Imaging process is generally defined as the mapping process of a scene (what you see in front, which is to be captured, through

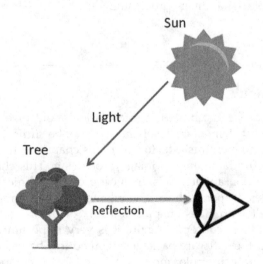

FIGURE 2.1
Fundamental principle of reflection.

the camera) to an image plane. (An image plane is the surface where the image is rendered.)

Image formation can be described as occurring in three phases. The first phase is the scene getting illuminated (lighted) by a source. In Figure 2.2 the light source is the sun. In the second phase, the scene that is illuminated reflects the radiations to the camera in focus (Figure 2.3). The third phase happens through the sensors in the camera, which can sense the radiations (Figure 2.4) completing the whole process.

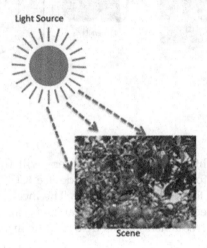

FIGURE 2.2
Image formation: Phase 1.

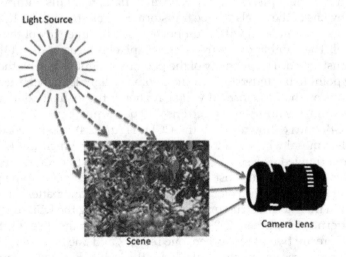

FIGURE 2.3
Image formation: Phase 2.

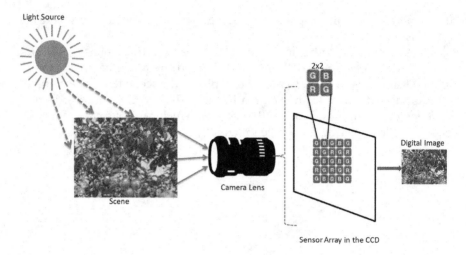

FIGURE 2.4
Image formation sequence.

The incoming light radiation to the camera will further be processed. This input is fed into the charge-coupled device (CCD), which is an array of sensors arranged together in a structure. The incoming light radiation is a mix of multiple frequencies. The sensor array is capable of collecting the red, blue, and green frequencies perfectly out of the incoming light radiation through the camera.

The CCD is a very sensitive photon detector. It is actually broken into smaller areas that can be used to build an image of the focused scene. A photon, a particle representing a quantum of light, that falls within the area defined by one of the pixels will be transformed to electrons, and the number of electrons accumulated will be proportional to the intensity of the scene at each pixel. The number of electrons in each pixel is measured and the scene gets reconstructed. The intensity of the photons of light falling on the CCD is the core point to be understood. If the photon of light is higher, the number of electrons on the CCD formed will be higher. If the intensity of the photon falling is mild, the number of electrons will be minimal.

The RGB matrix shown inside the CCD (Figure 2.4) is referred to as the Bayer filter mosaic. It is a color filter array (CFA) in which the RGB color filters are arranged as a square grid of photo sensors (the matrix-like structure). This setup is used most commonly in digital cameras to help in the process of creation of the color image. There is a unique pattern also being followed in this mosaic structure with respect to filling the RGB sensors. The filter pattern is 50% green, 25% red, and 25% blue (in the inset of the 2 × 2 matrix, there are two tiles of green, one red tile, and one blue tile). There are some alternate arrangements available for this setup. But, this Bayer filter is the most frequently followed pattern. The complete functioning of this module is explained next with appropriate examples.

FIGURE 2.5
Bayer mosaic.

Let us understand the functioning with a simple example. Assume that the incoming radiation is fed into the CCD array. The incoming radiation is a mixture of R, G, and B components. A sample Bayer filter pattern is presented in Figure 2.5. The incoming light will have the RGB components and the R filter will filter only the red components; the G filter does the same with the green components followed by the B filter with the blue components. The combination of the three together forms the image. One should remember that G is 50% of the total content, and the other two carry 25% each. Refer to Figure 2.6 to get a clear idea.

FOOD FOR THOUGHT

By now, you may have a query in mind. Why G is given more weight than R and B? What makes it so special?

Human eyes have greater sensitivity to the green color over red and blue. To replicate the same behavior, the Bayer filter is 50% green, while giving 25% each for blue and red.

The output from this phase, i.e., from the Bayer mosaic, is analog in nature and needs conversion. The conversion becomes mandatory as the analog signals cannot be processed digitally. Also, for storage it has to be a digital signal. Hence, the conversion from an analog to digital signal is mandatory. This is represented diagrammatically in Figure 2.7.

The continuous data has to be converted to the digital form with the following two steps:

a. Sampling – digitization of coordinate values.
b. Quantization – digitization of amplitude values.

For enhanced understanding of these two terms, see Figure 2.8.

Let's move on to the next topic of interest! The exciting journey has just begun.

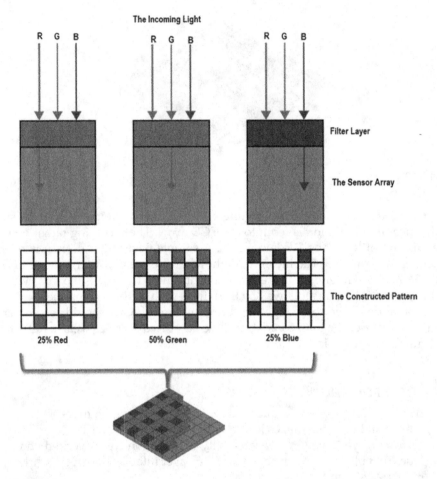

FIGURE 2.6
Image formation with Bayer filters.

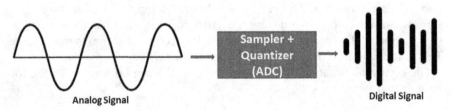

FIGURE 2.7
Analog to digital conversion.

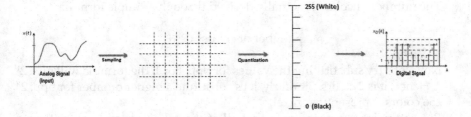

FIGURE 2.8
Quantization and sampling.

2.3 Bits per Pixel

A small introduction to pixels was provided in the previous chapter. Here, we will enhance the topic. Bits per pixel is normally abbreviated as bpp. It is the number of bits of information stored in each pixel of any image. People also define it as color depth. Yes, this has a strong connection with color.

The more the number of bits, obviously, one can expect more colors to be represented. But, as we know, this would require more memory for storage. As the image gets denser, it needs more memory. But the more the number of bits per pixel, the better the image quality.

The number of bits per pixel determines the number of colors to be accommodated in an image. See Table 2.1 for a reference.

TABLE 2.1

Bits Per Pixel versus Number of Colors

Bits per Pixel (bpp)	Number of Colors
1 bpp	2 colors
2 bpp	4 colors
3 bpp	8 colors
4 bpp	16 colors
5 bpp	32 colors
6 bpp	64 colors
7 bpp	128 colors
8 bpp	256 colors
10 bpp	1024 colors
16 bpp	65,536 colors
24 bpp	16,777,216 colors (16.7 million colors)
32 bpp	4,294,967,296 colors (4294 million colors)

The number of colors is actually derived through a simple formula:

$$\text{Number of colors} = 2^{bpp}$$

Now, let's try substituting the values for bpp. For 1, the formula will give 2^1 = 2. Hence, it is 2 colors. Similarly, let's substitute a higher number for bpp: 2^8 = 256 colors is present per pixel.

But, the point to remember is that all of the colors are none other than a variant (shade) of R, G, and B. This is how all colors are derived.

The next topic to be discussed is intensity.

2.4 Intensity, Brightness, and Contrast: Must-Know Concepts

You have come across the term *intensity* already. But, not in a technical manner as it has to be covered. The intensity of a pixel can be defined as the value corresponding to the pixel in consideration. If you refer to an 8-bit grayscale image, then there are 256 gray levels for any pixel considered. Let's refer to the grayscale image representation at this juncture. The shade for any pixel can range from 0 to 255, as represented in Figure 2.9.

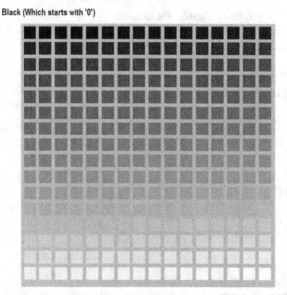

FIGURE 2.9
Image intensity. *Note*: All the boxes in the matrix represent the transition that happened from black to white.

Input Image

High brighness

Lower Brightness

FIGURE 2.10
Image brightness.

The next term in queue is *brightness*. Brightness is often confused with intensity. Brightness is a relative term. Let us assume there are three pixels with intensities 10, 50, and 255 and named X, Y, and Z, respectively. Now, how would we compare the brightness of these three? Simple, Z is the brightest of all the pixels. Y is brighter than X but not as bright as Z. Hence, it can be understood that the term brightness is relative. See the example representation presented in Figure 2.10 for better understanding.

The term *contrast* is equally important to be understood as well. Contrast is the difference between the minimum and the maximum pixel intensities in the considered image. Let us consider two images: Image X has a range of intensity from 20 to 80, and image Y having a range of intensity from 50 to 120. In this case, image Y has more contrast than image X. Also, to understand how the contrast plays a role in the image, refer to Figure 2.11.

2.5 Pixel Resolution and Pixel Density

Let us start with the term *pixel resolution* first. Most of you probably have experience with increasing/adjusting the pixel resolution of your computer screen. If not, we suggest you have a look at it now. Figure 2.12 refers to the Windows 7 resolution adjustment panel.

Input Image

High Contrast

Low Contrast

FIGURE 2.11
Image contrast.

Change the appearance of your display

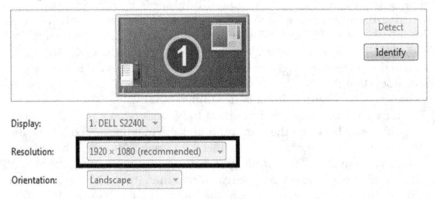

FIGURE 2.12
Resolution.

It is important to understand what pixel resolution actually is. Resolution normally refers to the size of the display in terms of the pixels. In the screenshot presented in Figure 2.12, the resolution is set as 1920 × 1080, that is, it has 1920 pixels horizontally and 1080 pixels vertically. So, in total 2,073,600 pixels are available in the display. It is a measure, but it does not guarantee the best display quality. There are many other parameters connected to the quality of an image, and resolution alone is not sufficient.

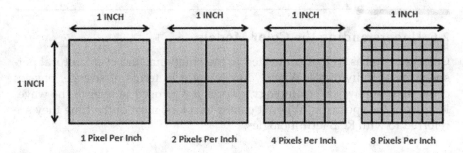

FIGURE 2.13
Pixel intensity.

TABLE 2.2

Pixel Density versus Pixels per Square Inch

Pixel Density (Pixels per Inch, ppi)	Pixels per Square Inch
1 ppi	1
2 ppi	4 (double ppi = quadruple pixel count)
4 ppi	16
8 ppi	64

The next related term to be understood is *pixel density*. Pixel density is often not given importance during discussions. But, it is very important and deserves more attention. Pixel density is the number of pixels present per inch on the display. The sharpness of the image is better with higher pixel density.

Let's now compare pixel resolution and pixel density. Resolution represents the number of pixels the image has. This includes the horizontal and the vertical planes, say 1920 × 1080, as shown in Figure 2.12. But pixel density is about how close each pixel is to another, which is represented as dots per inch (dpi). See Figure 2.13 to help understand the concept of pixel intensity.

The number of pixels in Figure 2.13 for 1 pixel per inch is 1, while for 2 pixels per inch it is 4 instead. From there on, the increase in incremental. Refer to Table 2.2, which shows how the count increases.

Note: When the pixel density is doubled, the information quadruples. That is, when 1 ppi increases to 2 ppi, the pixel density doubles and the pixel count quadruples.

Having discussed the concept of pixel density, it is time for us to move on to the next interesting topic.

2.6 Understanding the Color Models

Color is visual as well as connected to the emotional and even cultural perspectives of individuals. When you cite color in terms of science, physics
come first. In physics terminology, color is a way used to refer to the wavelengths in the spectrum. When it comes to colors, most of the time they are
referred to with RGB terminologies.

2.6.1 What Is a Color Model?

A color model can be defined as a system that makes use of the three primary colors (RGB) to produce a vast range of colors. There are many color
models used in the technology sector and each of them is different and has a
certain purpose. The range of colors that can be produced by deploying any
particular color model is referred to technically as a color space.

The different color models are:

1. RGB and CMY color models
2. HSV color model
3. YUV color model

Let's learn all of these, one after the another!

2.6.2 RGB Color Model and CMY Color Model

RGB is the standard for the primary colors, and, yes, whenever you talk or
hear about the color models, RGB comes first. Primary colors are used to
produce the secondary colors as and when required. Before dwelling deeper,
one should understand that there are two classifications of color models:
additive and subtractive models.

2.6.2.1 What Is an Additive Color Model?

The RGB color model is the finest example of an additive color model, as red,
green, and blue are added and brought together to produce a broad range of
other colors.

Going back to the RGB color model, using the primary colors R, G, and B in
several combinations with different levels of intensity, one can derive various
colors, naturally. One simple instance is how the color white is derived from
the RGB color model. If the light contains the combination of (additive)
red, green, and blue at equal strength, we get the color white (Figure 2.14).
To make it more technical, additive colors are all about adding individual
wavelengths. Various colors are derived through this process.

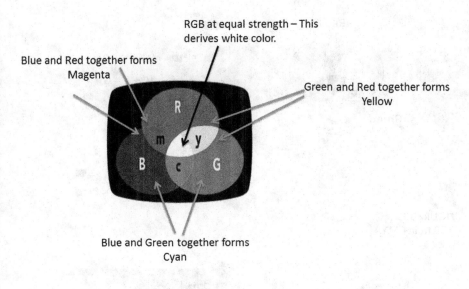

RGB at equal strength – This derives white color.

Blue and Red together forms Magenta

Green and Red together forms Yellow

Blue and Green together forms Cyan

Note: RGB – Primary Colors
CMY – Derived Colors

FIGURE 2.14
The color model fundamentals.

2.6.2.2 What Is a Subtractive Primary Color?

Subtractive colors are about the absorption or subtraction of certain wavelengths from white light, which acts as the input source.

When two of the three pure additive colors are combined, a new color is produced and it is referred to as a subtractive primary color. Using Figure 2.14, one can visualize when R and B are combined, it forms magenta; while R and G upon combining gives yellow; and finally, B and G when combined begets cyan (Figure 2.15). Cyan (C), magenta (M), and yellow (Y) are termed as subtractive primaries. They are also referred to as the CMY model.

To go further, magenta and yellow upon combination produces red, combining cyan and yellow gets you green, and cyan and magenta produces blue. Interestingly, Cyan + Magenta + Yellow = Black!

FOOD FOR THOUGHT

Can you name one application where these primitive and derived colors are used intensively?

All monitor and television displays use this concept!

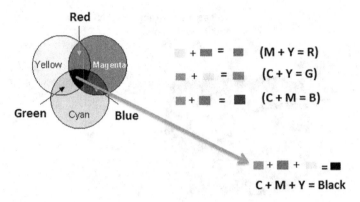

FIGURE 2.15
RGB from CMY.

| 0 | 60 | 120 | 180 | 240 | 300 | 360 |

FIGURE 2.16
Hue scale.

2.6.3 HSV Color Model

HSV corresponds to hue, saturation, and value. Some people call this HSB, which corresponds to hue, saturation, and brightness.

Just like RGB, the HSV color model is fundamentally composed of three components. They are as follows:

1. Hue – This is the color. It can be signified as a point in a 360-degree color circle (Figure 2.16).
2. Saturation – This is directly connected to the intensity of the color (range of gray in the color space). It is normally represented in terms of percentage ranging from 0% to 100%. If it is100%, it signifies an intense color presence.
3. Value – This can also be called brightness and just like saturation it is represented as percentage. The range is from 0% to 100%. Zero represents black and 100 represents the brightest.

The hue scale is presented in Figure 2.16 and it ranges from 0 to 360 degrees (also see Figure 2.17).

The next model to be discussed is the YUV model.

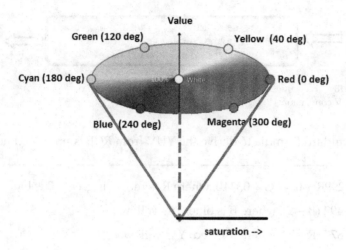

FIGURE 2.17
The HSV triangle.

2.6.4 YUV Color Model

YUV is one of the color encoding systems and is mostly used in the color image pipeline (i.e., components used between an image source [for example, a camera] and image renderer [any display device]). YUV is an alternate option for the traditional RGB in display systems and is one of the efficient options in an image processing application where displays are involved. In this color encoding scheme, the transmission errors are said to be reduced compared to the traditional RGB scheme. YUV standards have been globally accepted and products in the market almost are mostly in favor of YUV standards. Hence, this color model overtakes the rest of the schemes.

Here, it is important for readers to also understand two terms:

1. Luminance – This refers to the brightness.
2. Chrominance – This refers to the color.

In YUV, Y represents the luminance. U and V are connected to the chrominance, which refers to the color. Thus, people also refer to this color model as the luminance/chrominance color system. In this model, the luminosity of the given color is detached and the hue (color) is determined. The luminosity data goes into the Y channel, whereas U and V carries different content. The U channel is created after subtracting the Y from the amount of blue in the given image. Concerning V, this channel is created by subtracting the amount of red from Y.

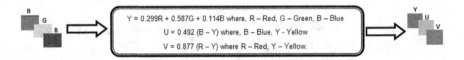

FIGURE 2.18
RGB to YUV conversion.

The standard formula to derive the YUV from RGB is presented next:

Y = 0.299R + 0.587G + 0.114B, where R is red, G is green, B is blue.

U = 0.492 (B − Y), where B is blue, Y is yellow.

V = 0.877 (R − Y), where R is red, Y is yellow.

Having said this, the conversion from the RGB to the YUV happens in the way as represented in Figure 2.18.

Is this done? No, we have more information to pay attention to.

There is a concept called chroma subsampling. What is chroma sub-sampling? Chroma subsampling is a process that is connected to the lessening of color resolution of video signals. The reason behind this is very straightforward: to save the bandwidth. Chroma is also called color component information. One can lessen or reduce this by sampling and thereby comes the term chroma subsampling. It happens by sampling at a lower rate than the brightness. As we know, brightness is all about luminance.

But, when the color information is reduced, won't it be detected by human eyes? The answer is interesting. Human eyes are more sensitive to brightness variation than to color variations and hence there is no problem!

Note: Readers should preferably read this topic twice to clearly understand.

Four different chroma sampling approaches are followed. They are 4:4:4, 4:2:2, 4:1:1, and 4:2:0. Let us understand these through the simple diagrammatic representation in Figure 2.19, which represents the color conversion for a 2 × 2 matrix, followed by the chroma subsampling models in Figures 2.20, 2.21, 2.22, and 2.23.

Variants for the YUV model are also available and they are:

1. YCbCr
2. YPbPr

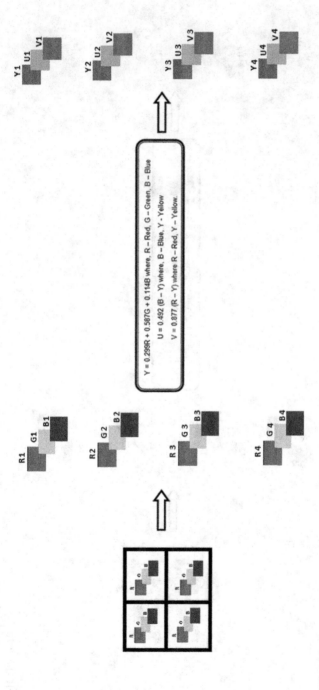

FIGURE 2.19
The RGB to YUV conversion process for 2 2 matrix.

40

Digital Image Processing

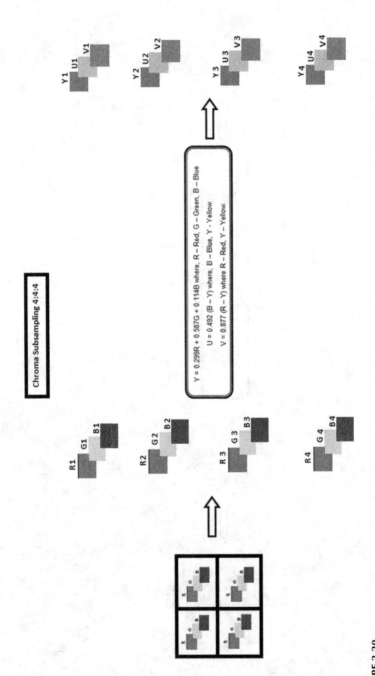

FIGURE 2.20
Chroma subsampling.

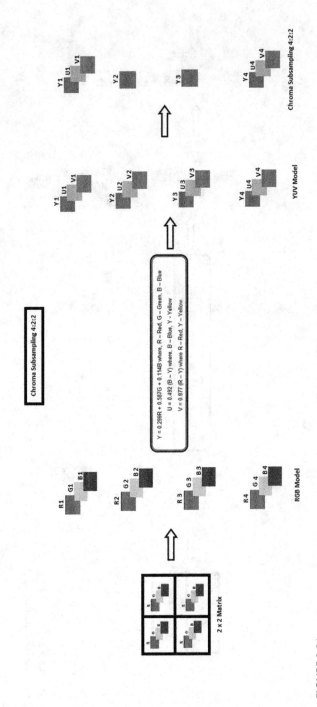

FIGURE 2.21
Chroma subsampling.

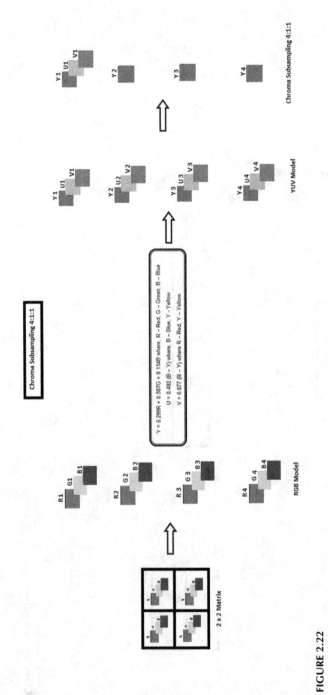

FIGURE 2.22
Chroma subsampling.

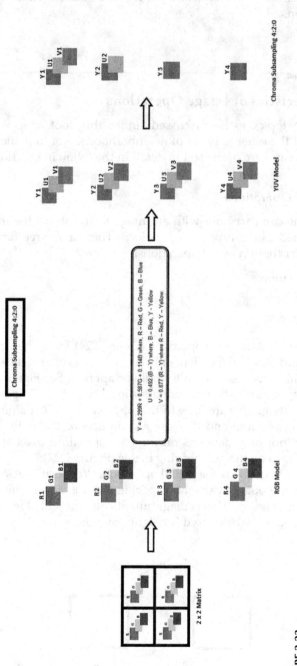

FIGURE 2.23
Chroma subsampling.

They are scaled versions of the YUV model, and hence, readers can pay less attention to them. The subsequent topic for discussion is characteristics of image operations.

2.7 Characteristics of Image Operations

There are two topics to be discussed under this roof. One is types of operations and the other is types of neighborhoods. Not to panic! Both are understandable and are discussed in detail in the following sections.

2.7.1 Types of Operations

The actions one can carry out with an image to transform the input to an output is defined as the types of operations. There are three fundamental categories under these types of operations:

1. Point operation
2. Local operator
3. Global operator

First, let's understand the point operation (Figure 2.24). Here, the output value at a specific coordinate is dependent only on the input value at the same coordinate and nothing else. An example would be apt here. See Figure 2.25.

The second operation to be understood is local operation. This is diagrammatically presented in Figure 2.26. In this approach, not just a pixel but the neighbors are considered and they are also in action. The output intensity level at a pixel not only depends on the corresponding pixel at the same coordinate but also on the neighboring pixels (Figure 2.27).

The next topic in queue is the global operation. What is it? Let's unfold the mystery! Here, the output value at a specific point is dependent on all the values in the input image. This is diagrammatically presented in Figure 2.28.

The next subject to be discussed is neighborhoods.

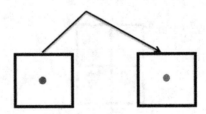

FIGURE 2.24
Point operation.

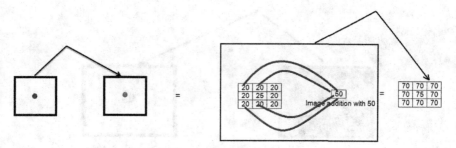

FIGURE 2.25
A simple example of point operation.

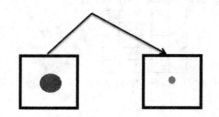

FIGURE 2.26
Local operation.

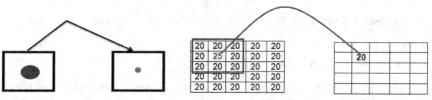

The cell with Value 25 is operated. But, that will be done considering the
neighboring cells too. i.e. average of the nearby cells in this case to alter that
25 to 20 has happened.

FIGURE 2.27
Local operation with an implementation example.

2.7.2 Types of Neighborhoods

As the name suggest, this concerns the neighboring pixels. Based on the
neighboring pixels, the value of the considered pixel is altered. There are
two types of neighborhoods supported in modern-day image processing.
They are:

- Rectangular sampling
- Hexagonal sampling

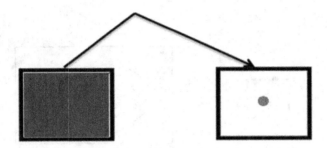

FIGURE 2.28
Global operation.

[North, South, East, West]

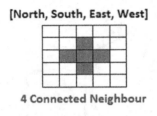

4 Connected Neighbour

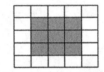

8 Connected Neighbour

[NorthEast, SouthEast, SouthWest, NorthWest, North, South, East, West]

FIGURE 2.29
Neighborhoods.

Let us start with rectangular sampling. In this method, normally a rectangle is laid over the image matrix and operations are done accordingly on the local neighbor. There are two subclassifications in this: the 4-connected neighbor and 8-connected neighbor techniques (Figure 2.29). Hexagonal sampling is not used much and is to be dealt with separately and hence we are ignoring it in this section.

2.8 Different Types of Image Formats

This is one of the topics that is part of any image processing book/playlist without fail because it carries much impact and importance.

Let's first define what image format is all about. It is a predefined and standard way of organizing a digital image. Also, image format is connected to how the image is stored. The format can be compressed or uncompressed and the same will be discussed in depth as follows for each image type.

The first image format to be discussed is the TIFF.

2.8.1 TIFF (Tag Image File Format)

TIFF is expanded as Tag Image File Format. It is normally referred to as a huge file format, meaning if an image is stored as a TIFF, it is expected to be huge in size. As we know, when an image gets larger, it has a lot of data and content in it. TIFF images are also classified as an uncompressed image format type. A TIFF is preferred where flexibility is paramount in terms of colors. TIFF can support grayscale, CMY, RGB, and more. TIFF is mostly preferred by graphic designers and photographers as it supports vast color options.

People also refer to TIFF as a lossless file format.

To understand TIFF better, the following pros and cons should be considered:

Pros

- Very versatile, and can support multiple colors and options such as CMY and RGB.
- Quality is not compromised and it ensures perfect and complete quality.

Cons

- Its very large size is a concern.

The next image type to be discussed is JPEG.

2.8.2 JPEG (Joint Photographic Experts Group)

Readers would have heard and may even be more familiar with the JPEG image type. Yes, it is very popular among all of us. Let us understand the technicalities of it.

The JPEG is extremely popular for many reasons. It is a compressed storage technique. Much information can be stored in the smaller sized file and hence it can save a lot of space. Your digital camera's default image type is likely JPEG as it gets better storage-related results.

Whereas the TIFF is lossless, the JPEG is lossy. It loses some information when compressed. The biggest concern with the JPEG image is the ability for the user to reedit images. You will not get the best quality when the JPEG image is edited, that is, the quality of the image is degraded. However, wherever the size of the image should be small (as in webpages) and needs to load faster, JPEG is the obvious choice.

Let's analyze the pros and cons of JPEGs:

Pros

- Small size and reduced storage needs.
- Default image type in digital cameras, which enables more photos to be stored.
- Apt for the websites and digital documents, as the image loads faster.
- Compatible with most operating systems and is widely accepted. In fact, this image type is indeed very popular.

Cons

- The discarded data is a huge concern. This could affect the content and quality.
- May create room for false observations because of artifacts.
- Transparency is hurt when this kind of image is used.

Next, let us discuss the GIF format.

2.8.3 GIF (Graphics Interchange Format)

GIF is expanded as Graphics Interchange Format. It is a fantastic and efficient image format. It has both the features of a JPEG and TIFF. Like the TIFF, GIF retains the quality, and like JPEG, it has a reduced storage scenario.

Yes, the GIF is a lossless compression technique-based image. It compresses the image, but with no loss. Hence, the size of the image is as small as a JPEG while the quality is retained.

But, there is a negative aspect to the GIF. It comes with very limited color range, meaning it may not support as many colors as desired. The compression happens by reducing the number of colors. To understand this better, if there are five shades of red, GIF would make it one shade of red.

The pros and cons are discussed next:

Pros

- Reduced size for file storage.
- Quality retainment.
- Suitable for images where multiple color shades are not required.

Cons

- Very limited color options.

The next type of file image to be discussed is PNG.

2.8.4 PNG (Portable Network Graphic)

The PNG solves some of the negative aspects identified with the GIF. The colors supported tend to be the major challenge in the GIF and they are addressed with a PNG. The complete range of colors is supported in a PNG. Even then, the competitor JPEG is in the driver's seat, because a PNG is a larger file when compared to JPEG and hence the preference for JPEG.

A PNG is classified as a lossless, compression-based image.

Pros

- Improved color range support compared to GIF.
- Increased transparency.
- Smaller file size than GIF.

Cons:

- File size still not smaller than JPEG.

The next type of image to be discussed is the RAW.

2.8.5 RAW Format

People refer to a "raw" format for a number of reasons. Raw image content is not processed and can't be used directly. Raw images are the format of the images immediately after creation, i.e., when you click a photo, before processing, it would be a raw image. Also, since it is not processed, a raw image cannot be printed. A RAW file is an uncompressed format, and since there has been no processing, the size of the file is very high.

There are many types of RAW formats available on the market. They include CR2 and CRW (both created by Canon), NEF (created by Nikon Cameras), and PEF (created by Pentax Digital Cameras).

The next topic of discussion is the fundamental steps in digital image processing.

2.9 Steps in Digital Image Processing

This is a very fundamental and very interesting topic for discussion. One should refer to the illustration in Figure 2.30 before going through the explanation.

The first step in digital image processing is image acquisition. We shall start with that.

1. Image acquisition.

   The first and foremost step is where to acquire the image. To make it a bit more technical, this stage is where the image is made

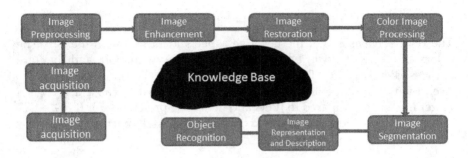

FIGURE 2.30
Steps in digital image processing.

available after a bit of preprocessing. Most of the time, the acquired image will be digital when it comes out the camera; if not, it should be converted to a digital image with the help of an analog-to-digital converter (ADC).

2. Image enhancement.

This is one of the most important steps in the entire workflow. If this step is done well, the rest of the steps should go good and meet expectations. The major focus of this step is to make sure that the image is good enough to be processed and has all that is needed to enable further processing. Here is when smoothing, sharpening, increasing/decreasing brightness, adjusting contrast, etc. all are carried out, which will facilitate the rest of the steps to come. This step is called "image enhancement", as it enhances the image in various aspects.

3. Image restoration.

Restoration is more connected to working with the appearance of the image, meaning this step helps in improving the appearance of the image. It is actually a step that can undo the defects in the image (degraded image). Degradation may also be in the form of, for example, noise or blurring, and restoration helps in restoring the image with better quality.

4. Color image processing.

In this step, the color information (R, G, B) can be used to extract and understand the features from the image. The features that one normally thinks of are color, texture, shape, and structure, and this enables the user to understand the image better for meaningful processing. There are multiple color conversion models available for use that can be used in this step.

5. Image segmentation.

As the very term *segmentation* means "partitioning", it is easier for one to understand what image segmentation could be. It is the process or the step through which a digital image is partitioned into multiple segments. This segmenting allows the user to identify the objects and to extract more meaningful information from the image. One can think of segmentation as a divide-and-conquer approach for the taken image. Segmentation divides the image into multiple segments and extracts the best out of it!

6. Image representation and description.

Immediately after segmentation, it is important to do further processing. It is not possible to just retain the same result of segmentation to arrive at meaningful results. Image representation is concerned with transforming the raw data arrived at after segmentation to some suitable form (feature vectors) for further processing. This can be achieved by two means:

- Boundary representation – Focus is on the external shape, for example, edges and corners.
- Regional representation – Focus is on the internal properties, such as texture and shape.

Readers need not worry much about these two now. They will be discussed in detail later.

Image description concerns feature selection. It helps in differentiation of object A from object B in the image.

7. Object recognition.

Recognition can be defined as the identification of someone or something from previous encounters or knowledge. This definition is perfect here. Recognition helps in recognizing what is what in the image. For instance, in an image that has a car and a motorcycle, the car will be recognized as a car and the motorcycle as a motorcycle. This is possible through the features present in the image.

Finally, there is one more term to be understood. It is knowledge base! *Knowledge base* is all about detailing the image. It helps in directing our focus to the region that has the information instead of searching all over. It is dependent on the problem statement. It could be searching for defects in textiles or it could be to segment some objects from a satellite image. Hence, knowledge base is all dependent on what you want to do with the image!

2.10 Elements of Digital Image Processing System

The previous topic was about the stages in the image processing, whereas in this section we are going to have a look at the components (hardware/sensor, etc.) deployed in the image processing system (Figure 2.31). Let us learn it this way.

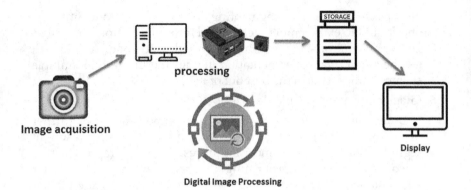

FIGURE 2.31
Components in digital image processing.

1. Components involved in the image acquisition stage.

    The major components involved in the image acquisition stage are

    a. Scanner

    b. Camera

    From the above two components, one can easily identify two sub-components. One is the sensor that senses the energy being radiated by the object that we want to capture (i.e., object of focus). The second one is the digitizer that converts the sensed image in the analog form to digital form, which would be apt for further processing.

2. Components involved in the processing stage.

    The computers or the workstation with appropriate software installed is the requirement. The current trends are toward smaller computing engines, which start from Raspberry Pi and go up to the Intel NUC and Intel AI Vision kit, which are very specific and rich in features, making them suitable for image processing applications.

3. Components for storage.

    This is one of the most important areas of concern when it comes to image processing. Mass storage is often required in image processing applications. Based on the application being developed, one can choose any of the following storage options:

    a. Cases where faster processing is required, i.e., real time, one can store the images in the memory available on the processor itself or can store them at the next level through memory cards, which are in closer proximity to the processor. But the size of the memory available in the processor is normally not large, and hence this option should be preferred wherever real speed is required. However, the images should later be stored in secondary storage medium for future usage.

b. Online storage options are on the rise these days. One can even store images in the cloud and processing can be done there as well. But cost factors are to be considered in this option. One may have to spend for this storage. Also, if images are secured and has confidential content, remote storage may not be preferred.

c. Storing the images after processing for future reference is called archiving. The images when stored after processing fall under this category and can be carried out through secondary storage devices like drives.

4. Components involved in the display.

The most preferred displays include monitors, projectors, printers, and television screens.

In this chapter we have revisited the concepts behind image formation, types of images, and quantization and sampling. In the next chapter, let's focus our attention toward the noise in an image, the types of image noise, and also the possible remedial measures to subdue them.

2.11 Quiz

1. Human eyes are the inspiration for the camera's invention. True or false?
2. What is the basic principle behind capturing any image?
3. The _____ mosaic has the combination of RGB.
4. In the Bayer mosaic, R is ___%, G is ___%, and B is ___ %.
5. The reason for having green color sensors with 50% weightage in the Bayer mosaic is _____.
6. Bpp stands for _____.
7. Brightness is _____.
8. _____ is the difference between the minimum and the maximum pixel intensities in an image.
9. _____ can be defined as a system that makes use of the three primary colors (RGB) to produce a vast range of colors.
10. _____ normally refers to the size of the display in terms of the pixels.
11. _____ is the finest example of an additive color model, where red, green, and blue are added together to produce a broad range of other colors.

12. _____ is all about measuring/understanding how close each pixel is to one another.
13. Expand HSV.
14. Hue represents color. True or false?
15. Value represents contrast. True or false?

2.11.1 Answers

1. True
2. Reflection
3. Bayer
4. 25, 50, and 25
5. To replicate the human eye's sensitivity to green
6. Bits per pixel
7. Relative
8. Contrast
9. Color model
10. Resolution
11. RGB color model
12. Pixel density
13. Hue, saturation, and value
14. True
15. False

2.12 Review Questions

1. Describe the fundamental principle behind image formation with an appropriate figure.
2. Draw the sequence involved in image formation, technically.
3. What is the Bayer mosaic and how does it work?
4. Define bits per pixel.
5. Define brightness.
6. Define contrast.
7. Define resolution.
8. What is pixel density?
9. Differentiate resolution and pixel density.

10. Define color model.

11. What are the color models discussed in this chapter?

12. What is an additive color model?

13. What is a subtractive color model?

14. Can you name one application where primary and derived colors are used intensively?

15. What is the H, S, and V in the HSV color model?

16. Define luminance and chrominance.

17. What is chroma subsampling?

18. What are the major technical steps involved in digital signal processing? Present diagrammatically.

19. What are the major components involved in digital signal processing?

2.12.1 Answers

1. When a light ray falls on any object, the basic tendency is to reflect it back. We should realize that the eyes have a lens as well, just like a camera, and this is the fundamental principle.

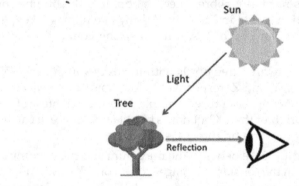

2.

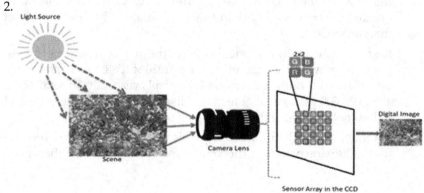

3. The incoming light has RGB components. The R filter will filter only the red component, and the G filter and B filter do the same with their respective components. The combination of the three together forms the image. One should remember that G is 50% of the total content, whereas the two others contain 25% each.

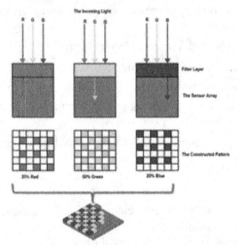

4. Bits per pixel is normally abbreviated as bpp. It is the number of bits of information stored in each pixel of any taken image. People also define it as color depth. Yes, it has a strong connection with color.

5. Let us assume there are three pixels with intensities 10, 50, and 255 and are named X, Y, and Z, respectively. Now, how would we compare the brightness of these three? Simple, Z is the brightest of all the pixels. Y is brighter than X but not as bright as Z. Hence, it can be understood that the term brightness is relative.

6. Contrast is the difference between the minimum and the maximum pixel intensities in the considered image. Let us consider two images. Image X has the range of intensity from 20 to 80. Image Y has range of intensity from 50 to 120. In this case, image Y has more contrast than image X.

7. Resolution normally refers to the size of the display in terms of pixels. For a screen with the resolution set as 1920 × 1080, the arrangement has 1920 pixels horizontally and 1080 pixels vertically. In total, there are 2,073,600 pixels available in the display. It is only a measure and it does not guarantee the best display quality.

8. Pixel density is the number of pixels present per inch on the display. The sharpness of the image is better with a higher pixel density.

9. Resolution represents the number of pixels the image has. This includes the horizontal and the vertical planes, say 1920 × 1080. Pixel density is how close each pixel is to one another, which is represented as dots per inch (dpi).

10. A color model can be defined as a system that makes use of the three primary colors (RGB) to produce a vast range of colors.

11. RGB color model/CMY color model, HSV color model, YUV color model.

12. The RGB color model is the finest example of an additive color model, as red, green, and blue are added together to produce a broad range of other colors.

13. Subtractive colors are about absorption or subtraction of certain wavelengths from white light, which acts as the input source. Cyan, magenta, and yellow are termed as subtractive primaries. This is also referred to as the CMY model.

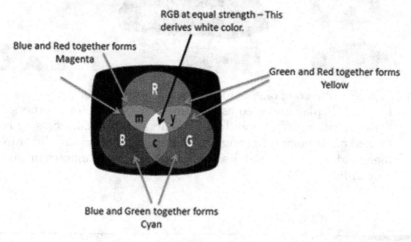

14. All monitors and the television displays use this concept!

15. HSV:

- Hue – The color. It is signified as a point in a 360-degree color circle.

- Saturation – This is directly connected to the intensity of the color (gray range in the color space). It is normally represented in terms of percentage. The range is from 0% to 100%, where 100% signifies intense color.

- Value – This can also be called brightness and just like saturation it is represented as a percentage. The range is from 0% to 100%, where 0% represents black and 100% represents the brightest.

16. Luminance refers to the brightness and chrominance refers to the color.

17. Chroma subsampling is a process that is connected to the lessening of color resolution of video signals to save bandwidth. Chroma is also called color component information. One can lessen or reduce this by sampling and hence the term chroma subsampling. It happens by sampling at a lower rate than the brightness. As we know, brightness is all about luminance.

18.

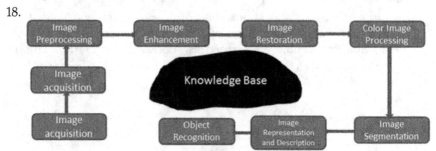

19. Typically, the components for image acquisition, storage, processing, and display are rated as the core components in the process. For acquisition, it starts with the sensors or camera. Processing is carried out in computing engines. Storage can be done locally or in the cloud. Screens, monitors, and projectors are examples of display units.

Further Reading

Adelson, E.H., Anderson, C.H., Bergen, J.R., Burt, P.J. and Ogden, J.M., 1984. Pyramid methods in image processing. *RCA Engineer*, 29(6), pp. 33–41.

Baxes, G.A., 1984. *Digital image processing: A practical primer.* Cascade Press.

Ibraheem, N.A., Hasan, M.M., Khan, R.Z. and Mishra, P.K., 2012. Understanding color models: A review. *ARPN Journal of Science and Technology*, 2(3), pp. 265–275.

Miano, J., 1999. *Compressed image file formats: Jpeg, png, gif, xbm, bmp.* Addison-Wesley Professional.

Plataniotis, K.N. and Venetsanopoulos, A.N., 2013. *Color image processing and applications.* Springer Science & Business Media.

Russ, J.C., 2016. *The image processing handbook.* CRC Press.

Solomon, C. and Breckon, T., 2011. *Fundamentals of digital image processing: A practical approach with examples in Matlab.* John Wiley & Sons.

Walmsley, S.R., Lapstun, P. and Silverbrook Research Pty Ltd, 2006. Method and apparatus for Bayer mosaic image conversion. U.S. Patent 7,061,650.

Walmsley, S.R., Lapstun, P. and Silverbrook Research Pty Ltd, 2006. Method for Bayer mosaic image conversion. U.S. Patent 7,123,382.

Webb, J.A., 1992. Steps toward architecture-independent image processing. *Computer,* 25(2), pp. 21–31.

3

Image Noise: A Clear Understanding

Learning Objectives

After reading this chapter, the reader should have a clear understanding about:

- Noise in an image
- Types of image noise
- How noise is created in an image?
- Remedial measures possible for noise

3.1 Introduction

It is always important to understand a definition first before diving deep into a subject. This chapter is intended to create complete awareness about image noise, its types, and related concepts.

Image noise is defined in the literature as "a variation or deviation of brightness or color information in images". Image noise is often referred to as digital noise. The source of image noise is often camera sensors and associated internal electronic components. These components in cameras introduce anomalies or imperfections in the image that certainly degrade the quality of the image. These imperfections are referred to as image noise. Figure 3.1 is an image with no noise and Figure 3.2 has noise introduced to the image. One can see the significant impact of noise on the image.

Generally, noise appears in an image because of any one or many of the following reasons:

- Insufficient lighting
- Environmental conditions

DOI: 10.1201/9781003217428-3

- Sensor temperature
- Transmission channels
- Dust factors

The factors that influence image noise are depicted in Figure 3.3.

We will first cover the types of noise an image can be affected with. A simple diagrammatic representation is presented in Figure 3.4.

The first type of noise to be discussed will be photoelectronic noise.

FIGURE 3.1
Image without noise.

FIGURE 3.2
Image with noise.

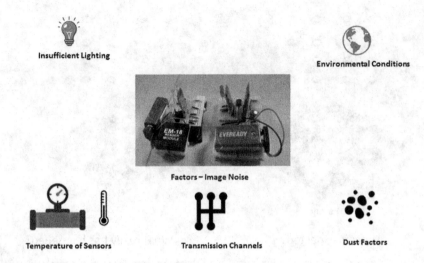

FIGURE 3.3
Factors influencing image noise.

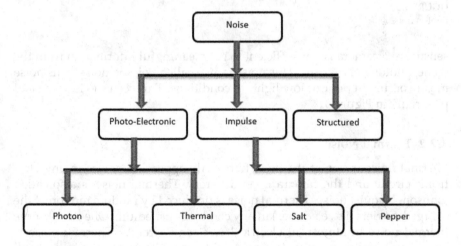

FIGURE 3.4
Types of image noise.

3.2 Photoelectronic Noise

Photoelectronic noise includes photon noise and thermal noise. The following sections will elaborate on both.

3.2.1 Photon Noise (Also Called Shot Noise or Poisson Noise)

Photon noise is a type of noise connected to the uncertainty associated with the measurement of light. When the number of photons sensed by the

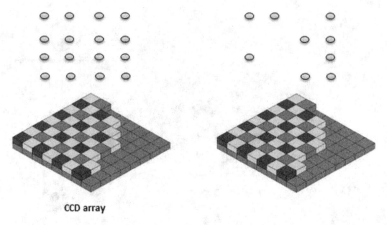

CCD array

What is expected?

Even distribution of the photons has
happened in this case.

What really has happened?

It has become random and effect of
photons has not been proper.

FIGURE 3.5
Photon noise.

sensors in a camera is not sufficient to get meaningful information from the
scene, photon noise arises. This noise is also called Poisson noise. This noise
mostly occurs in poor or low lighting conditions. This scenario is presented
pictorially in Figure 3.5.

3.2.2 Thermal Noise

Thermal noise is one of the most frequently appearing noises in any electronic circuit and the camera is no different. Thermal noise is also called
Johnson–Nyquist noise. Thermal noise is produced by random motion of the
charged carriers (i.e., electrons) in any conducting medium. One can observe
thermal noise in almost all electrical/electronic circuits. Thermal noise is
also known as white noise. It is referred to as white noise as it impacts all
the frequency components of the signal equally. Thermal noise naturally
increases with temperature. Try this out in MATLAB with the code snippet
in Figure 3.6. The image has to be fed in as input in the code.

The original image without noise (input image) is presented in Figure 3.1,
compared to the impact of this noise presented in Figure 3.7.

3.2.3 How to Overcome Photoelectronic Noise?
   (Thermal Noise/Photon Noise)

There are no proven methods to eliminate photon noise. Photon noise, as discussed, is directly related to the photons recorded in the real image. A bright

```
% imread is the function for image read.
% imnoise is the function for introducing noise
% based on arguments passed, noise will be induced.

I = imread('Input_image.png');
figure,imshow(I)

C = imnoise(I,'localvar',rand(1,100),rand(1,100));
figure,imshow(C)
```

FIGURE 3.6
MATLAB code snippet.

FIGURE 3.7
Impact of thermal noise

image will have many photons and therefore little photon noise. A dim or dull image has more photon noise as it may not have many photons in action. This kind of noise cannot be known or corrected in advance. Also, it is to be clearly observed that photon noise is not related to the equipment or electronics associated with it. It is totally dependent on the number of photons. To conclude, the larger the number of photons collected, the lesser the noise.

Thermal noise can be reduced with careful reduction of temperature of operation. Also, thermal noise gets reduced with a reduction of the resistor values in the circuit.

3.3 Impulse Noise

The next type of noise one should know is impulse noise. One type of impulse noise is salt-and-pepper noise.

Impulse noise is one of the noises that has always received a lot of attention from researchers. It is often regarded as a very important source for corrupting digital images. After going through the literature, it is understood that many models for impulse noise reduction has been proposed and still it is thought that there is a lot of room for improvement.

Image impulse noise mainly arises due to the missed transmission of signals. The literature confirms that this type of noise can also be caused due to malfunctioning of the pixels in the sensors of the camera or memory location faults in storage.

Impulse noise is also called spike noise and independent noise. The name "independent" has been given owing to the nature of noise. It has the tendency to change or modify the pixel values independently, thereby creating the damage.

3.3.1 Salt-and-Pepper Noise

Salt-and-pepper noise is peculiar. In this type of noise, the images have dark pixels in the bright regions and bright pixels in the dark regions. The main source and origin of this kind of noise is through analog-to-digital converter errors. As cited earlier, bit transmission errors also cause salt-and-pepper noise. The resulting impact is the image has a lot of black and white spots. The noisy pixel in this noise type would have either a salt value or pepper value. The salt value has a gray level of 255 (brightest) and the pepper value has a gray level of 0 (darkest). The MATLAB code for introducing salt-and-pepper noise is presented in Figure 3.8. The input image is presented as in Figure 3.1. Figure 3.9 is the result after introducing salt-and-pepper noise.

3.3.2 How to Overcome Impulse Noise?

Impulse noise can be overcome with filters, such as median filters and mean filters. Also, dark frame subtraction can be carried out to remove impulse noise. Details of all the filters and noise removal techniques are dealt with in Chapter 4.

```
% imread is the function for image read.
% imnoise is the function for introducing noise (here, salt and pepper)
% based on arguments passed, noise will be induced.
I = imread('Input_Image.png');
figure,imshow(I)

J = imnoise(I,'salt & pepper',0.02);
figure, imshow(J)
```

FIGURE 3.8
MATLAB code snippet for introducing salt-and-pepper noise.

FIGURE 3.9
Salt-and-pepper noise.

3.4 Structured Noise

Structured noise can be periodic stationary or periodic nonstationary in nature. Or it can be aperiodic.

With periodic nonstationary noise, the noise parameters, including amplitude, frequency, and phase, are varied across the image. This is mostly caused by interference between the electronic components or electrical components.

For periodic stationary noise, the noise parameters – amplitude, frequency and phase – are fixed, unlike with nonstationary noise. Interference between the components causes this noise, as with nonstationary noise.

When an image is affected by periodic noise, it appears like a repeating pattern added on top of the original image. When someone wants to analyze in the frequency domain, it appears like discrete spikes. Notch filters are used to minimize the impact of the periodic noise.

If the noise is aperiodic, the pattern in the image is repetitive in nature.

The code for inducing structured noise is presented in Figure 3.10, and the results obtained upon running the code are also presented in Figure 3.11 and Figure 3.12.

In this chapter we have focused on noise in an image, the types of noise, and the possible ways to overcome them. Let's proceed to the next chapter to further understand the importance of edge detection in image processing, various edge detection operators, and also the pros and cons of various edge detection techniques.

```matlab
I = imread('IMage.png');
figure,imshow(I)
grayImage = rgb2gray(I);

% Add big ripples to it.
rowVector = (1 : rows)';
period = 10; % 20 rows
amplitude = 0.5; % Magnitude of the ripples.
offset = 1 - amplitude; % How much the cosine is raised above 0.
cosVector = amplitude * (1 + cos(2 * pi * rowVector / period))/2 + offset;
ripplesImage = repmat(cosVector, [1, columns]);
minValue = min(min(ripplesImage))
maxValue = max(max(ripplesImage))
figure,imshow(ripplesImage, [0 maxValue]);

% Multiply the ripples by the image to get an image with periodic "noise" in it.
grayImage = ripplesImage .* double(grayImage);
minValue = min(min(grayImage))
maxValue = max(max(grayImage))
figure,imshow(grayImage, [0 255]);
```

FIGURE 3.10
MATLAB code snippet for inducing structured noise.

FIGURE 3.11
Ripples to be injected in the original image as noise.

FIGURE 3.12
The structured noise effect

3.5 Quiz

1. _____ is a variation or deviation of brightness or color information in an image.
2. The source of the image noise is mostly from _____.
3. Which of the following are sources of noise?
   a. Insufficient lighting
   b. Environmental conditions
   c. Sensor temperature
   d. All the above
   e. None of the above
4. Photon noise is also called _____.
5. _____ noise is created with the uncertainty associated with the measurement of light.
6. Photon noise is fully dependent on _____.
7. _____ is produced by random motion of the charged carriers (called electrons) in any conducting medium.
8. Image impulse noise mainly arises due to the _____.

3.5.1 Answers

1. Noise
2. Camera sensors and electronic components
3. d. All the above
4. Shot noise or Poisson noise
5. Photon noise
6. Number of photons falling on the charge-coupled device (CCD) of the camera.
7. Thermal noise.
8. Missed transmission of signals.

3.6 Review Questions

1. Define noise with respect to images.
2. What are the major types of noise identified with respect to images?

3. What is photon noise?

4. How can photon noise be eliminated?

5. What is salt-and-pepper noise? How is it created?

6. What are the ways to curtail salt-and-pepper noise?

7. What are the types of structured noise?

3.6.1 Answers

1. Image noise is defined as "a variation or deviation of brightness or color information in images".

2. Refer to Figure 3.4.

3. Photon noise is a type of noise connected to the uncertainty associated with the measurement of light. When the number of photons sensed by the sensors from the camera is not sufficient to get meaningful information from the scene, photon noise arises.

4. There are no proven methods to eliminate photon noise. Photon noise is directly related to the photons recorded in the real image. A bright image has many photons and therefore little photon noise. A dim or dull image has more photon noise as it might not have many photons in action.

5. In this type of noise, the images have dark pixels in the bright regions and bright pixels in the dark regions. The main source and origin of this kind of noise is through analog-to-digital converter errors.

6. Filters, including median filters and mean filters, can be used to curtail salt-and-pepper noise.

7. Structured noise can be periodic stationary or periodic nonstationary in nature. Or it can even be aperiodic as well.

Further Reading

Boncelet, C., 2009. Image noise models. In *The essential guide to image processing* (pp. 143–167). Academic Press.

Mastin, G.A., 1985. Adaptive filters for digital image noise smoothing: An evaluation. *Computer Vision, Graphics, and Image Processing*, 31(1), pp. 103–121.

Narendra, P.M., 1981. A separable median filter for image noise smoothing. *IEEE Transactions on Pattern Analysis & Machine Intelligence*, 1, pp. 20–29.

Peters, R.A., 1995. A new algorithm for image noise reduction using mathematical morphology. *IEEE Transactions on Image Processing*, 4(5), pp. 554–568.

Rank, K., Lendl, M. and Unbehauen, R., 1999. Estimation of image noise variance. *IEE Proceedings – Vision, Image and Signal Processing, 146*(2), pp. 80–84.

Toh, K.K.V., Ibrahim, H. and Mahyuddin, M.N., 2008. Salt-and-pepper noise detection and reduction using fuzzy switching median filter. *IEEE Transactions on Consumer Electronics, 54*(4), pp. 1956–1961.

4

Edge Detection: From a Clear Perspective

Learning Objectives

After reading this chapter, the reader should have a clear understanding about:

- Definition of edge detection
- Importance of edge detection in image processing
- Edge detection operators
- What edges are?
- Why detect edges?
- Types of edges
- Sobel operator
- Prewitt operator
- Robinson compass mask
- Krisch compass mask
- Canny operator
- Laplacian operator
- Comparison of edge detection operators

4.1 Introduction

What is edge detection? This question has to be answered before going deeper into the topic.

Edges are defined as "sudden and significant changes in the intensity" of an image. These changes happen between the boundaries of an object in an image. In Figure 4.1, the mug is seen in the input image, and once the edges are detected, one can find out the exact layout or boundary of the object. The edges are detected based on the significant change in intensity between the

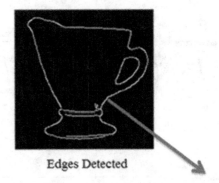

Input Image   Edges Detected

Edges in Image (Sudden change in
the intensity can be seen, object gets
detected from there)

FIGURE 4.1
What are edges?

objects in the image. To be precise, the mug has a different intensity from the
gray background and it is the key idea for us to identify the edges. So, if there
are many objects in an image, edges are the easiest way to identify all of them.

4.2 Why Detect Edges?

There are many reasons for detecting the edges and they include the
following:

1. One can understand the shape of objects in the image only when the
   edges are detected. So, ideally to understand an object and its shape,
   it becomes inevitable for someone to detect the edges.
2. There are many technical issues and challenges mapped to the segmentation, registration, and object identification techniques. Edges
   prove to be efficient with these techniques at fundamental levels.

4.3 Modeling Intensity Changes/Types
    of Edges: A Quick Lesson

As discussed at the beginning of this chapter, edges are the sudden and significant changes in the intensity of an image. The significant change in the

image intensity can be seen as a discontinuity, as it is a variation from the regular flow. There are four types of edges/discontinuities. They are:

a. Step edges/discontinuity
b. Line edges/discontinuity
c. Ramp edges/discontinuity
d. Roof edges/discontinuity

We shall understand all these one after another with appropriate diagrammatic support.

a. Step edges – In step edges type, the image intensity unexpectedly and sharply changes from one value to another, as shown Figure 4.2. It looks similar to the step/pulse, and hence is regarded as the step edges.

b. Line edges – This is almost like the step edge. But, there is one main difference. The image intensity sharply changes from one value to another, but it will return to the starting value soon in a shorter span of distance. This can be understood clearly by referring to Figure 4.3.

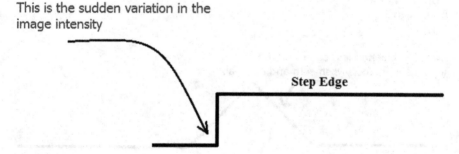

This is the sudden variation in the image intensity

Step Edge

FIGURE 4.2
Step edge.

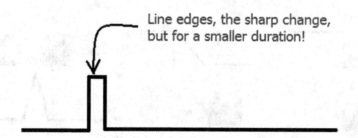

Line edges, the sharp change, but for a smaller duration!

FIGURE 4.3
Line edge.

c. Step edges are noted as ramp edges when the intensity changes are not immediate but occur over a finite distance gradually for a longer duration/distance (Figure 4.4).

d. Line edges are noted as roof edges when the intensity changes are not immediate but occur over a finite distance gradually for a longer duration/distance (Figure 4.5).

The edge types are shown in relation to image intensity changes in Figure 4.6.

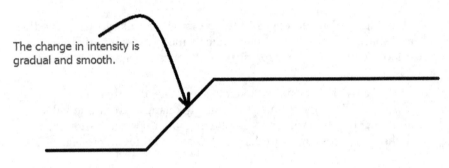

FIGURE 4.4
Ramp edge.

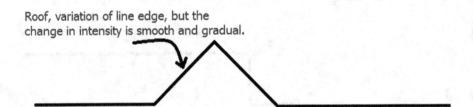

FIGURE 4.5
Roof edge.

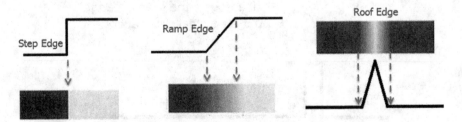

FIGURE 4.6
Types of edges.

4.4 Steps in Edge Detection

Any process has to follow a sequence and edge detection is no different. There are three steps followed in edge detection process (Figure 4.7):

1. Image smoothing
2. Edge points detection
3. Edge localization

Let us expand on these steps to impart clarity.

1. Image smoothing is the removal of the noise from the image. In addition, the removal or suppression of the noise should be done in such a way that the quality of the image is not altered. Essentially, image smoothing is making the image noise-free. See Figure 4.8.
2. Edges are detected through identifying the sudden changes in the intensity. Even noise is all about sudden change in the intensity. Edge points detection is a process where the noise alone is carefully removed or discarded, retaining the edges (Figure 4.9).

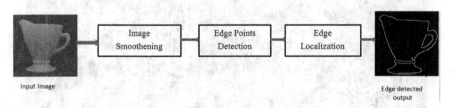

Input Image → Image Smoothening → Edge Points Detection → Edge Localization → Edge detected output

FIGURE 4.7
Steps in edge detection.

FIGURE 4.8
Image smoothing.

FIGURE 4.9
Edge points detection.

FIGURE 4.10
Edge localization.

    3. The final step in the sequence is edge localization. Sometimes processes like thinning and linking are to be carried out to accurately locate the edges. This process is called edge localization (Figure 4.10).

Now, it is the time to understand all the available and frequently used edge detection algorithms. We will start with the Sobel operator.

4.5 Sobel Operator

Using the Sobel edge detector, the image is processed in the X and Y directions. This would result in the formation of new image, which actually is the sum of the X and Y edges of the image. This approach works through calculation of the gradient of the image intensity at every pixel within the image.

Let's get into the math. The Sobel filter has two kernels (3 × 3 matrix). One of them correspond the X (horizontal) and the other shall be used for the Y (vertical) direction. These two kernels should be convoluted with the original image under process and through which the edge points are calculated with ease. An example is presented below. The kernel values shown are fixed for Sobel filter and cannot be altered.

The Gaussian filter plays a vital role in the entire process. The fundamental idea behind the Gaussian filter is the center having more weight than the rest. The general approach for detecting the edges is with the first-order or second-order derivatives as shown in Figure 4.11.

A 1D Gaussian Filter can be either $\begin{vmatrix} 1 \\ 2 \\ 1 \end{vmatrix}$ or $\overline{\begin{array}{ccc} 1 & 2 & 1 \end{array}}$ for the following forms to find Sobel-X or Sobel-Y.

The next sequence is to convolute the Gx (Sobel-X) and Gy (Sobel-Y) over the input image, which shall enable us to calculate the value for one pixel at a

$$\begin{vmatrix} 1 \\ 2 \\ 1 \end{vmatrix} * \overline{\begin{array}{ccc} 1 & 0 & -1 \end{array}} = \begin{vmatrix} 1 & 0 & -1 \\ 2 & 0 & -2 \\ 1 & 0 & -1 \end{vmatrix}$$

1D Gaussian Filter   **x - Derivative**   **Sobel - X**

$$\begin{vmatrix} 1 \\ 0 \\ -1 \end{vmatrix} * \overline{\begin{array}{ccc} 1 & 2 & 1 \end{array}} = \begin{vmatrix} -1 & -2 & -1 \\ 0 & 0 & 0 \\ 1 & 2 & 1 \end{vmatrix}$$

y - Derivative   **1D Gaussian Filter**   **Sobel - Y**

FIGURE 4.11
Sobel-X and Sobel-Y.

time. Then, the shift happens and the move has to be made toward the right, i.e., the next column shift to the column end. A similar process is followed for the row shifting from top to bottom. Remember, for columns it is left to right movement, whereas for rows it is top to bottom movement with the Gx and Gy. The is mathematically explained next with the aid of Figure 4.12.

The matrix in Figure 4.12a is a 5 × 4 image that is being convoluted with the Gx (Sobel-X) operator. In the considered 5 × 4 matrix, we take only the first 3 × 3 matrix, in which the center value (I) is computed.

Upon the convolution, the resultant matrix in Figure 4.12b should be obtained.

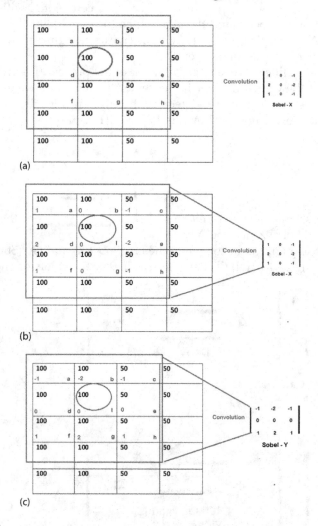

FIGURE 4.12
(a) In the given 5 × 4 image being convoluted with the Gx (Sobel-X) operator, we take only the first 3 × 3 matrix and the center value (I) is computed. (b) Upon convolution, this resultant matrix Gx shall be obtained. (c) The resultant matrix Gy upon convolution.

The Sobel-X values are convoluted with the original image matrix values. Hence, the resultant matrix values would be as follows:

Gx = 1 * a + 0 *b + (–1) * c + 2 * d + (–2) * e + 1*f + 0 * g + (–1) * h
   = 1 * 100 + 0 * 100 + (–1) * 50 + 2 * 100 + (–2) * 50 + 1 * 100 + 0 * 100 + (–1) * 50
   = 200

Similarly, Gy has to be found (Figure 4.12c). Going by the same calculations we have done for Gx, Gy can be computed.

Gy = (–1) * a + (–2) * b + (–1) * c + 0 * d + 0 * e + 1 * f + 2 * g + 1 * h
   = (–1) * 100 + (–2) * 100 + (–1) * 50 + 0 * 100 + 0 * 50 + 1 * 100 + 2 * 100 + 1 * 50
   = 0

The preceding calculations should help in visualizing the edges indirectly. In the x-axis there are changes in the cells. But, in the y-axis there are no changes and hence the result Gy is 0.

The resulting gradient approximation can be calculated with

$$G = \sqrt{G_X{}^2 + G_Y{}^2}$$

The *G* will be compared against the threshold and with which one can determine whether the taken point is an edge .

The implementation of Sobel edge detections in MATLAB is presented next with the aid of Figures 4.13, 4.14, and 4.15.

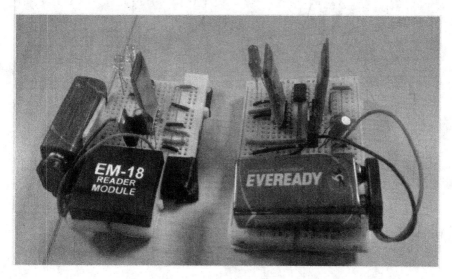

FIGURE 4.13
Input image.

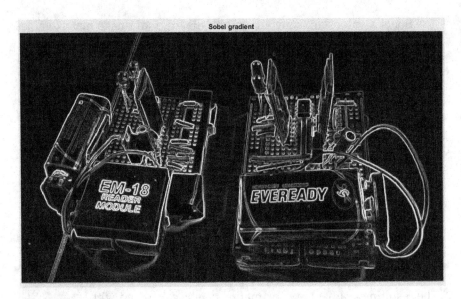

FIGURE 4.14
The midway results – gradient magnitude – of the implementation of Sobel edge detections in MATLAB.

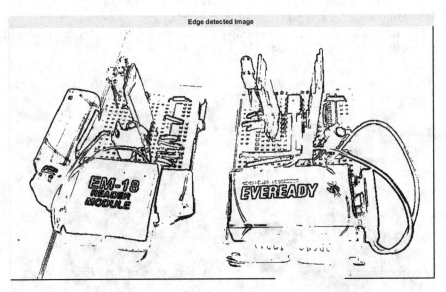

FIGURE 4.15
The final detected edges of the implementation of Sobel edge detections in MATLAB.

The MATLAB code for Sobel edge detection is presented in the following:

```
A=imread('InputImage.png');
B=rgb2gray(A);
figure,imshow(B)

C=double(B);
for i=1:size(C,1)-2
  for j=1:size(C,2)-2
    %Sobel mask for x-direction:
    Gx=((2*C(i+2,j+1)+C(i+2,j)+C(i+2,j+2))-(2*C(i,j+1)
    +C(i,j)+C(i,j+2)));
    %Sobel mask for y-direction:
    Gy=((2*C(i+1,j+2)+C(i,j+2)+C(i+2,j+2))-(2*C(i+1,j)
    +C(i,j)+C(i+2,j)));

    %The gradient of the image
    %B(i,j)=abs(Gx)+abs(Gy);
    B(i,j)=sqrt(Gx.^2+Gy.^2);
  end
end
figure,imshow(B); title('Sobel gradient');

Thresh=100;
B=max(B,Thresh);
B(B==round(Thresh))=0;

B=uint8(B);
figure,imshow(~B);title('Edge detected Image');
```

```
The next operator to be learned is Prewitt edge
detector.
```

4.6 Prewitt Edge Detector

The Prewitt edge detector is like the Sobel edge detection but with a minor change. The Prewitt operator gives the values that are symmetric around the center, whereas the Sobel operator gives weight to the point that is lying closer to (x, y).

The Prewitt x and y operator values are as follows:

$$\begin{vmatrix} 1 & 0 & -1 \\ 1 & 0 & -1 \\ 1 & 0 & -1 \end{vmatrix}$$

Prewitt – X

$$\begin{vmatrix} -1 & -1 & -1 \\ 0 & 0 & 0 \\ 1 & 1 & 1 \end{vmatrix}$$

Prewitt – Y

The implementation and code for the Prewitt x and y operators are as follows:

```
A=imread('InputImage.png');
B=rgb2gray(A);
figure,imshow(B)

C=double(B);

for i=1:size(C,1)-2
  for j=1:size(C,2)-2
    %Sobel mask for x-direction:
    Gx=((1*C(i+2,j+1)+C(i+2,j)+C(i+2,j+2))-(1*C(i,j+1)
    +C(i,j)+C(i,j+2)));
    %Sobel mask for y-direction:
    Gy=((1*C(i+1,j+2)+C(i,j+2)+C(i+2,j+2))-(1*C(i+1,j)
    +C(i,j)+C(i+2,j)));
    %The gradient of the image
    %B(i,j)=abs(Gx)+abs(Gy);
    B(i,j)=sqrt(Gx.^2+Gy.^2);

  end
end
figure,imshow(B); title('Prewitt Gradient');

Thresh=100;
B=max(B,Thresh);
B(B==round(Thresh))=0;

B=uint8(B);
figure,imshow(~B);title('Edge detected Image');
```

The results are presented in Figures 4.16, 4.17, and 4.18.

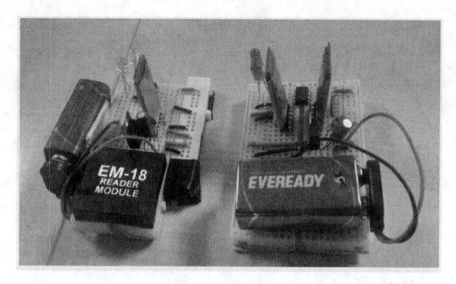

FIGURE 4.16
Input image.

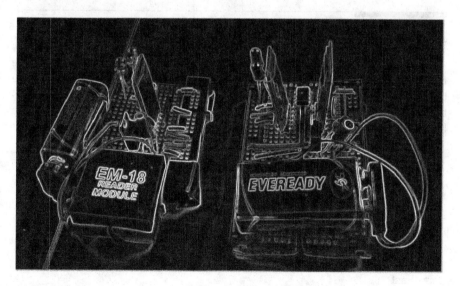

FIGURE 4.17
The Prewitt gradient.

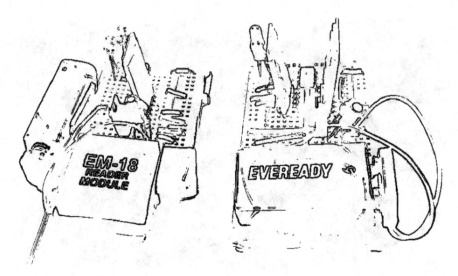

FIGURE 4.18
Detected edges.

4.7 Robinson Edge Detector

Another edge detection algorithm is the Robinson compass mask. The reason behind the "compass" name is simple. In this approach, we take one mask and rotate it in all possible eight directions and hence it is regarded as a compass mask. The compass directions considered are listed as follows:

- North
- North west
- West
- South west
- South
- South east
- East
- North east

The masks are frames, as was discussed earlier for the Sobel operator. Figure 4.19 shows the mask matrices for the directions.

The results obtained are presented in Figures 4.20 and 4.21.

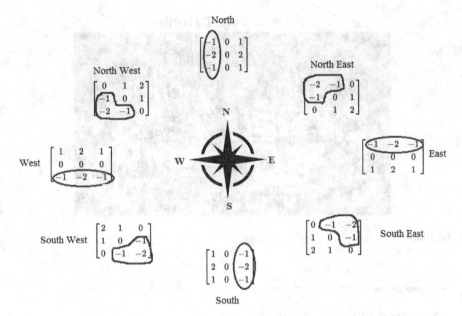

FIGURE 4.19
Robinson mask.

FIGURE 4.20
Input image.

The procedure, i.e., mathematical approaches, to be followed with the input image matrix remains the same as for the Sobel operator. Readers are expected to follow the same approach to detect the edges.

The Robinson mask is the same as the Krisch compass mask but with a very minor difference, as explained next.

Robinson Edge Detection

FIGURE 4.21
Output image.

4.8 Krisch Edge Detector

Every aspect of the Krisch edge detector remains the same as for afore-mentioned detectors other than the aspect of changing the mask as per the requirements in the Krisch edge detector. This is more flexible compared to the Robinson mask.

The eight directions are:

- North
- North west
- West
- South west
- South
- South east
- East
- North east

The corresponding mask structure is presented in Figure 4.22.

The MATLAB code and the result obtained while using the Krisch edge detector is presented next.

```
clear all;
clc;
close all;
bw4=imread('IMage.png');
bw4=rgb2gray(bw4);
```

```
figure(1)
imshow(bw4)
title('Input Image')

t=1200 ;
bw5=double(bw4);
[m,n]=size(bw5);
g=zeros(m,n);

for i=2:m-1
  for j=2:n-1
  d1 = (5*bw5(i-1,j-1)+5*bw5(i-1,j)+5*bw5(i-1,j+1)-3*bw5
  (i,j-1)-3*bw5(i,j+1)-3*bw5(i+1,j-1)-3*bw5(i+1,j)-3
  *bw5(i+1,j+1))^2;
  d2 = ((-3)*bw5(i-1,j-1)+5*bw5(i-1,j)+5*bw5(i-1,j+1)-3*
  bw5(i,j-1)+5*bw5(i,j+1)-3*bw5(i+1,j-1)-3*bw5(i+1,j)-
  3*bw5(i+1,j+1))^2;
```

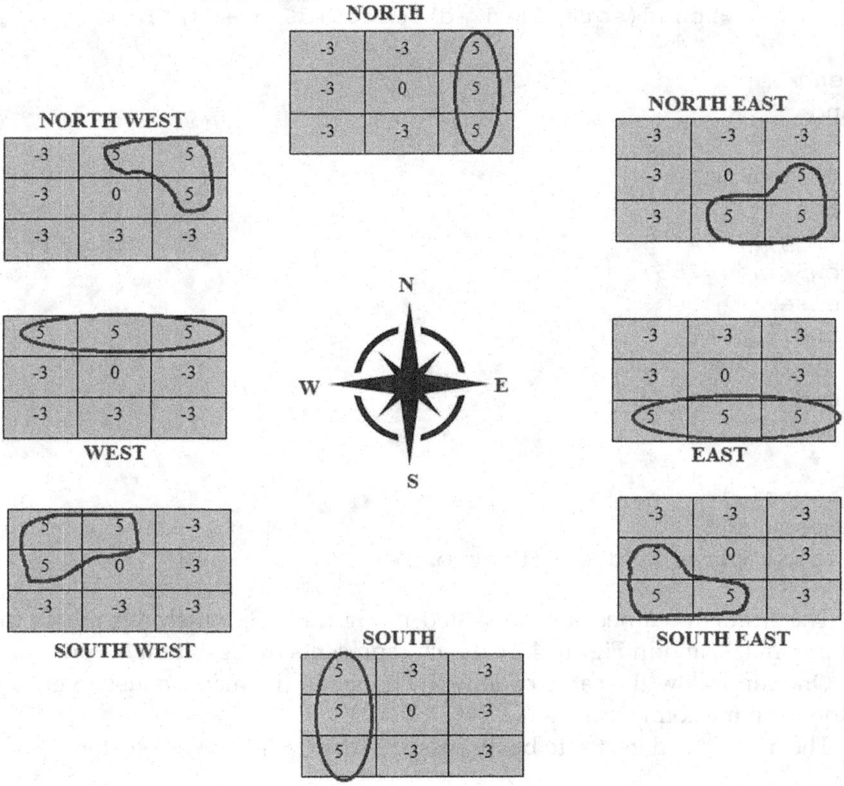

FIGURE 4.22
Krisch mask structure.

```
d3 =((-3)*bw5(i-1,j-1)-3*bw5(i-1,j)+5*bw5(i-1,j+1)-3*
bw5(i,j-1)+5*bw5(i,j+1)-3*bw5(i+1,j-1)-3*bw5(i+1,j
)+5*bw5(i+1,j+1))^2;
d4 =((-3)*bw5(i-1,j-1)-3*bw5(i-1,j)-3*bw5(i-1,j+1)-3*
bw5(i,j-1)+5*bw5(i,j+1)-3*bw5(i+1,j-1)+5*bw5(i+1,j
)+5*bw5(i+1,j+1))^2;
d5 =((-3)*bw5(i-1,j-1)-3*bw5(i-1,j)-3*bw5(i-1,j+1)-3*
bw5(i,j-1)-3*bw5(i,j+1)+5*bw5(i+1,j-1)+5*bw5(i+1,j
)+5*bw5(i+1,j+1))^2;
d6 =((-3)*bw5(i-1,j-1)-3*bw5(i-1,j)-3*bw5(i-1,j+1)+5*
bw5(i,j-1)-3*bw5(i,j+1)+5*bw5(i+1,j-1)+5*bw5(i+1,j
)-3*bw5(i+1,j+1))^2;
d7 =(5*bw5(i-1,j-1)-3*bw5(i-1,j)-3*bw5(i-1,j+1)+5*bw5
(i,j-1)-3*bw5(i,j+1)+5*bw5(i+1,j-1)-3*bw5(i+1,j)-3
*bw5(i+1,j+1))^2;
d8 =(5*bw5(i-1,j-1)+5*bw5(i-1,j)-3*bw5(i-1,j+1)+5*bw5
(i,j-1)-3*bw5(i,j+1)-3*bw5(i+1,j-1)-3*bw5(i+1,j)-3
*bw5(i+1,j+1))^2;
g(i,j)=round(sqrt(d1+d2+d3+d4+d5+d6+d7+d8));

 end
end

for i=1:m
 for j=1:n
 if g(i,j)>t
 bw5(i,j)=255;
 else
 bw5(i,j)=0;
  end
 end
end

figure(2)
imshow(bw5)
title('kirsch Edge Detection')
```

The results obtained are presented in Figure 4.23, which represents the input image, and in Figure 4.24, which represents the resultant output.

One can follow the same code with change in the mask values to get the Robinson mask implemented.

The next edge detector to be discussed is the Canny edge detector.

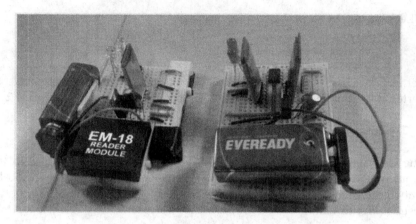

FIGURE 4.23
Input image.

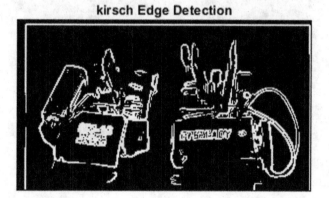

FIGURE 4.24
Resultant output image.

4.9 Canny Edge Detection

The Canny edge detector is not like other traditional edge detectors; it is just not masking or hovering on the input image matrix. Instead, it is detailed and has steps to follow. This section will clearly explain those steps.

Canny edge detection technique is more than just a plain edge detection technique. It also suppresses the noise while flawlessly detecting the edges.

Let's go step by step:

1. Conversion to grayscale.

Let us take a sample image and proceed with the conversion. We have converted the input RGB image (Figure 4.25) to a grayscale image (Figure 4.26).

2. Gaussian blur.

The Gaussian blur is an operator that helps in removing the noise in the input image. This noise-removed image enables further processing to be smooth and flawless. The sigma value has to be appropriately set for better results (Figure 4.27).

FIGURE 4.25
Input image.

FIGURE 4.26
Grayscale converted image result.

3. Intensity gradient calculation.

Let's go back to the basics. The Sobel filter is to be used in this process. Let's understand what an edge is all about. Sudden intensity change is the edge and, in fact, the intensity change of the pixel is the edge.

Next, the Sobel operator has to be applied over the input image, and the steps and sequences remain the same as per the process explained for Sobel edge detection. The resultant Sobel-operated image is presented in Figure 4.28 and is referred to as the gradient magnitude of the image.

FIGURE 4.27
Gaussian blur operated image.

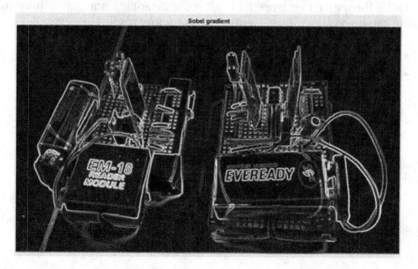

FIGURE 4.28
The Sobel gradient.

We preferred the Sobel operator, which is the general approach. But, it is not the rule to always go with Sobel operator. It can be any gradient operator and the result should be the gradient magnitude of the image.

The resulting gradient approximation can be calculated with

$$G = \sqrt{G_X^2 + G_Y^2}$$

The G will be compared against the threshold, with which one can determine if the taken point is an edge or not.

The formula for finding the edge direction is Theta = inv tan (Gy/Gx).

1. Non-maximum suppression.Non-maximum suppression is the next step in the sequence. The gradient magnitude operators discussed in the previous stage normally obtain thick edges. But, the final image is expected to have thin edges. Hence, the process of non-maximum suppression should enable us to derive thin edges from thicker ones through the following procedure.

We have the edge direction already available to us. The subsequent step is to relate the identified edge direction to a direction that can be sketched in the image, i.e., ideally, it is a prediction of how the movement of edges could happen.

An example is always handy and we have taken a 3 × 3 matrix as a reference. It's all about the colors and Figure 4.29 is to be visualized as a 3 × 3 matrix for the scenario being discussed.

The possible directions of movement are presented in Figure 4.30. The center cell is the region of interest for us. It is important to understand this point. There can be only four possible directions for any pixel. They are:

- 0 degrees
- 45 degrees

FIGURE 4.29
A 3 × 3 matrix example.

- 90 degrees
- 135 degrees

Hence, it forces us into a situation where the edge has to be definitely oriented toward one of these four directions. This is a kind of approximation. For example, if the orientation angle if observed to be 5 degrees , it is taken as 0 degrees. Similarly, if it is 43 degrees, it should be rounded off to 45 degrees.

For ease of understanding we have drawn a semicircle with color shading that represents 180 degrees (Figure 4.31). (But, the actual scenario is for 360 degrees.)

With Figure 4.31 as reference, the following rules are stated:

1. Any edge that comes under the yellow range is set to 0 degrees (which means from 0 to 22.5 degrees and 157.5 to 180 degrees are set to 0 degrees).

2. Any edge that comes under the green range is all set to 45 degrees (which means 22.5 degrees to 67.5 degrees is set as 45 degrees).

3. Any edge coming under the blue range is all set to 90 degrees (which means 67.5 degrees to 112.5 degrees is set as 90 degrees).

4. Any edge coming under the red range is all set to 135 degrees (which means 112.5 degrees to 157.5 degrees is set as 135 degrees).

After this process, the direction of the edges is mapped to any of the four directions mentioned earlier. The input image now should look like the one

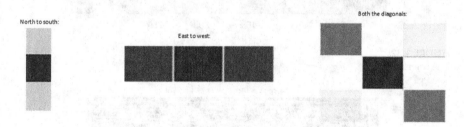

FIGURE 4.30
The possible directions of movement.

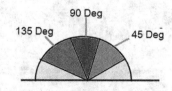

FIGURE 4.31
A semicircle is drawn with color shading that represents 180 degrees. (But, the actual scenario is for 360 degrees.)

presented in Figure 4.32 where directions of the edges are appropriately mapped.

The last step in the process comes now. The edge directions are all determined and the non-maximum suppression is to be applied. Non-maximum suppression, as the name suggests, is a process where suppression of the pixels to zero that cannot be considered as an edge is carried out. This shall enable the system to generate a thin line in the output image as shown in Figure 4.33. These results are obtained before the thresholding and, as expected, the next stage is to perform thresholding and smoothing.

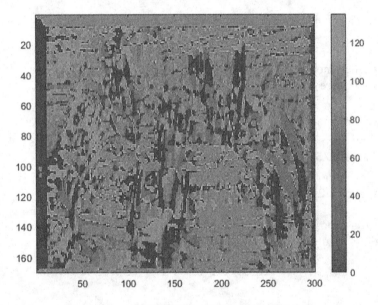

FIGURE 4.32
The color map.

FIGURE 4.33
Results before double thresholding.

5. Thresholding: A must-do process.

As one could see from the previous stage's results, non-maximum threshold-ing has not provided us excellent results. There is still some noise. The image even raises a thought in mind that some of the edges shown may not really be there and some edges could be missed in the process. Hence, there has to be a process to address this challenge. The process to be followed is thresholding.

We need to go with double thresholding and in this process we have to set two thresholds: one high and another low. Assume a high threshold value as 0.8. Any pixel with a value above 0.8 is to be seen as a stronger edge. The lower threshold can be 0.2. In that case, any pixel below this value is not an edge at all and hence set them all to 0.

Now comes the next question: What about the values in between, from 0.2 to 0.8? They may or may not be an edge. They are referred as weak edges. There has to be a process to determine which of the weak edges are actual edges so as to not to miss them.

6. Edge tracking.

As discussed in the previous step, it is important for us to now understand which of the weaker edges are actual edges. A simple approach may be fol-lowed. We can call the weak edges connected to strong edges as strong/actual edges and retain them. Weak edges that are not connected to stronger ones are to be removed.

7. The final cleansing.

All the remaining weak edges can be removed and that is it. The process is complete. Once this process is done, we should get the output image in Figure 4.34.

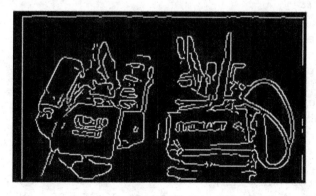

FIGURE 4.34
Final result with edges detected.

The MATLAB code for the Canny edge detection is presented below:

```
clear all;
clc;
%Input image
img = imread ('IMage.png');
%Show input image
figure, imshow(img);
img = rgb2gray(img);
figure, imshow(img);
img = double (img);
%Value for Thresholding
T_Low = 0.075;
T_High = 0.175;
%Gaussian Filter Coefficient
B = [2, 4, 5, 4, 2; 4, 9, 12, 9, 4;5, 12, 15, 12, 5;4,
9, 12, 9, 4;2, 4, 5, 4, 2 ];
B = 1/159.* B;
%Convolution of image by Gaussian Coefficient
A=conv2(img, B, 'same');
A=uint8(A)
figure,imshow(A);
%Filter for horizontal and vertical direction
KGx = [-1, 0, 1; -2, 0, 2; -1, 0, 1];
KGy = [1, 2, 1; 0, 0, 0; -1, -2, -1];
%Convolution by image by horizontal and vertical filter
Filtered_X = conv2(A, KGx, 'same');
Filtered_Y = conv2(A, KGy, 'same');
%Calculate directions/orientations
arah = atan2 (Filtered_Y, Filtered_X);
arah = arah*180/pi;
pan=size(A,1);
leb=size(A,2);
%Adjustment for negative directions, making all
directions positive
for i=1:pan
  for j=1:leb
    if (arah(i,j)<0)
      arah(i,j)=360+arah(i,j);
    end;
  end;
end;
arah2=zeros(pan, leb);
%Adjusting directions to nearest 0, 45, 90, or 135
degree
```

```
for i = 1 : pan
  for j = 1 : leb
    if ((arah(i, j) >= 0 ) && (arah(i, j) < 22.5) ||
(arah(i, j) >= 157.5) && (arah(i, j) < 202.5) ||
(arah(i, j) >= 337.5) && (arah(i, j) <= 360))
      arah2(i, j) = 0;
    elseif ((arah(i, j) >= 22.5) && (arah(i, j) < 67.5)
|| (arah(i, j) >= 202.5) && (arah(i, j) < 247.5))
      arah2(i, j) = 45;
    elseif ((arah(i, j) >= 67.5 && arah(i, j) < 112.5)
|| (arah(i, j) >= 247.5 && arah(i, j) < 292.5))
      arah2(i, j) = 90;
    elseif ((arah(i, j) >= 112.5 && arah(i, j) < 157.5)
|| (arah(i, j) >= 292.5 && arah(i, j) < 337.5))
      arah2(i, j) = 135;
    end;
  end;
end;
figure, imagesc(arah2); colorbar;
%Calculate magnitude
magnitude = (Filtered_X.^2) + (Filtered_Y.^2);
magnitude2 = sqrt(magnitude);
BW = zeros (pan, leb);
%Non-Maximum Supression
for i=2:pan-1
  for j=2:leb-1
    if (arah2(i,j)==0)
      BW(i,j) = (magnitude2(i,j) == max([magnitude2(i,j),
magnitude2(i,j+1), magnitude2(i,j-1)]));
    elseif (arah2(i,j)==45)
      BW(i,j) = (magnitude2(i,j) == max([magnitude2(i,j),
magnitude2(i+1,j-1), magnitude2(i-1,j+1)]));
    elseif (arah2(i,j)==90)
      BW(i,j) = (magnitude2(i,j) == max([magnitude2(i,j),
magnitude2(i+1,j), magnitude2(i-1,j)]));
    elseif (arah2(i,j)==135)
      BW(i,j) = (magnitude2(i,j) == max([magnitude2(i,j),
magnitude2(i+1,j+1), magnitude2(i-1,j-1)]));
    end;
  end;
end;
BW = BW.*magnitude2;
figure, imshow(BW);
%Hysteresis Thresholding
T_Low = T_Low * max(max(BW));
```

```
T_High = T_High * max(max(BW));
T_res = zeros (pan, leb);
for i = 1 : pan
  for j = 1 : leb
    if (BW(i, j) < T_Low)
      T_res(i, j) = 0;
    elseif (BW(i, j) > T_High)
      T_res(i, j) = 1;
    %Using 8-connected components
    elseif ( BW(i+1,j)>T_High || BW(i-1,j)>T_High ||
BW(i,j+1)>T_High || BW(i,j-1)>T_High || BW(i-1, j-1)>T_
High || BW(i-1, j+1)>T_High || BW(i+1, j+1)>T_High ||
BW(i+1, j-1)>T_High)
      T_res(i,j) = 1;
    end;
  end;
end;
edge_final = uint8(T_res.*255);
%Show final edge detection result
figure, imshow(edge_final);
```

Up to this section, we have used first-order derivatives for edge detection. Now, it is time to learn second-order derivatives.

4.10 Laplacian: The Second-Order Derivatives

There are some new terms we are going to learn in this section. Stay tuned.

What we normally look for is the peaks in the image. We do not actually worry much about the color content. As discussed in the previous sections, if there is a steeper change or a sharp change in the intensity, we declare it as an edge. This is found to be a nice approach right? But, there are challenges.

We have seen so far that declaring some point as a peak or not is a tough call. Thresholding comes to the rescue such that above the threshold we call it a peak and below that we ignore it. Let us refer to Figure 4.35. One could see that on the left to the curve, where exactly the curve starts rising, the slope is definitely positive. Coming to the right side, the slope is negative and this does not require any explanation. Hence, it is very obvious that there should a zero crossing, which is noted in the figure. That is the point that reveals the edge location. The Laplacian edge detector uses this as its basis.

The Laplacian edge detector uses only one kernel, whereas it was two with respect to the Sobel edge detector. The Laplacian edge detector is capable of calculating the second-order derivative in a single go. The following are the kernels used.

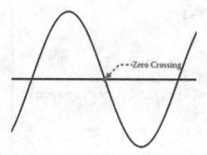

FIGURE 4.35
Zero crossing.

The following kernel focuses on horizontal and vertical directions alone:

0	−1	0
−1	4	−1
0	−1	0

The following kernel focuses on all the directions including diagonals:

−1	−1	−1
−1	8	−1
−1	−1	−1

The process remains the same as we did with the other edge detectors. With the above, two kernel operations can be done.

The MATLAB code and the sample results for this edge detector are presented next:

```
clear
clear all;
a=imread('IMage.png');
a=rgb2gray(a);
[r c]=size(a)
a=im2double(a);
%filter=[0 -1 0;-1 4 -1; 0 -1 0];
filter=[-1 -1 -1;-1 8 -1; -1 -1 -1];
result=a;
for i=2:r-1
  for j=2:c-1
    sum=0;
    row=0;
    col=1;
```

```
      for k=i-1:i+1
      row=row+1;
      col=1;

      for l=j-1:j+1
        sum = sum+a(k,l)*filter(row,col);
        col=col+1;
      end
    end
  result(i,j)=sum;
  end
end
figure, imshow(result);
```

Figures 4.36 and 4.37 reveal the edges for the input images through usage of the two aforementioned kernels.

There are, however, some disadvantages to the Laplacian approach:

1. There are two pixel thick edges produced (refer to Figures 4.36 and 4.37).

2. Very highly sensitive to noise.

Table 4.1 compares the various edge detections techniques, and lists the pros and cons of each technique.We have learned the importance of edge detection in image processing and related topics in this chapter. Now it's time to explore frequency domain, and the significant role played by different filters on a sample image along with their comparison. Let's move on to the next chapter.

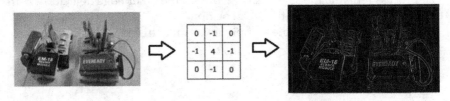

FIGURE 4.36
Edge detection – Kernel 1.

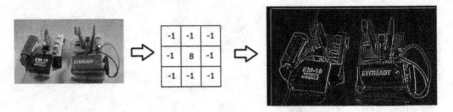

FIGURE 4.37
Edge detection – Kernel 2.

TABLE 4.1

Comparison of Edge Detection Techniques

Edge Detector	Crisp Note	Parameter	Advantages	Disadvantages
Sobel	No detailed information is fetched using this edge detector.	Threshold	• Simple approach. • Closest approximation to the gradient magnitude. • Edge detections happen alongside the orientation.	• More sensitive to noise. • Edges detected are still inaccurate.
Prewitt	Better sensitivity to horizontal and vertical edges.	Threshold	• Simple approach. • Edge detections happen alongside the orientation.	• More sensitive to noise. • Edges detected are still inaccurate.
Robinson	Compass masked-based approach.	Threshold	Maximum edge strength can be found.	Requires more time for calculation.
Krisch	• Compass masked-based approach. • Flexible compared to Robinson approach.	Threshold	Maximum edge strength can be found.	Though more flexible than Robinson, it still requires more time for calculation.
Canny	Most dominantly used than other edge detectors.	Non-maximum suppression and thresholding	Signal-to-noise ratio has improved. Improved detection of edges even in noise conditions.	Complex and tedious computation process.
Laplacian	Zero crossing is the fundamental concept.	Second-order derivative	Computationally faster and produces exceptional results with better input quality.	• There are two pixel thick edges produced in this method. • Very highly sensitive to noise.

4.11 Review Questions

1. Define edges.
2. What is the actual need to detect edges?
3. What are the four types of edges discussed in this chapter?
4. Define step edge.
5. Define ramp edge.
6. What are three important steps in the edge detection process?
7. What is image smoothing?
8. How is the Sobel operator different from the Prewitt?
9. What is a Robinson compass mask?
10. How is a Robinson mask different from the Krisch edge detector?
11. What are the major disadvantages of the Laplacian edge detector?

4.11.1 Answers

1. Edges are "sudden and significant changes in the intensity" of an image. These changes happen between the boundaries of an object in an image. (a) One can understand the shape of objects in the image only when the edges are detected. So, ideally to understand an object and its shape, it becomes inevitable for someone to detect the edges. (b) There are many technical issues and challenges mapped to the segmentation, registration, and object identification techniques. Edges prove to be efficient with these techniques at the fundamental levels.

2. Step edges/discontinuity, line edges/discontinuity, ramp edges/discontinuity, roof edges/discontinuity.

3. Here in this type, the image intensity unexpectedly and sharply changes from one value to another. It looks similar to the step/pulse and hence is regarded as the step edges.

4. Step edges shall be framed as ramp edges, although the intensity changes are not immediate but occur over a finite distance gradually for a longer duration/distance.

5. Image smoothing, edge points detection, edge localization.

6. Image smoothing is all about removal of noise from an image. In addition, the removal or suppression of the noise should be done in such a way that the quality of the image is not altered. Essentially, image smoothing is all about making the image noise-free.

7. The Prewitt edge detector is similar to the Sobel edge detector but with a minor change. The Prewitt operator gives the values that are symmetric around the center. But the Sobel operator gives weight to the point that is lies closer to (x, y).

8. The reason behind the name is simple. In this approach, we should take one mask and rotate it in all possible eight directions and hence it is regarded as a compass mask. The compass directions considered are north, north west, west, south west, south, south east, east, and north east.

9. The edge detector is again used for finding edges like the Robinson edge detector. Every feature remains the same other than the aspect of changing the mask as per the requirements in the Krisch edge detector. This is more flexible compared to the Robinson mask.

10. The major disadvantages of the Laplacian edge detector are (a) there are two pixel thick edges produced in this method and (b) it is very highly sensitive to noise.

Further Reading

Canny, J., 1986. A computational approach to edge detection. *IEEE Transactions on Pattern Analysis and Machine Intelligence*, 6, pp. 679–698.

Gupta, S. and Mazumdar, S.G., 2013. Sobel edge detection algorithm. *International Journal of Computer Science and Management Research*, 2(2), pp. 1578–1583.

Jin-Yu, Z., Yan, C. and Xian-Xiang, H., 2009, April. Edge detection of images based on improved Sobel operator and genetic algorithms. In *2009 International Conference on Image Analysis and Signal Processing* (pp. 31–35). IEEE.

Lindeberg, T., 1998. Edge detection and ridge detection with automatic scale selection. *International Journal of Computer Vision*, 30(2), pp. 117–156.

Marr, D. and Hildreth, E., 1980. Theory of edge detection. *Proceedings of the Royal Society of London. Series B. Biological Sciences*, 207(1167), pp. 187–217.

Torre, V. and Poggio, T.A., 1986. On edge detection. *IEEE Transactions on Pattern Analysis and Machine Intelligence*, 2, pp. 147–163.

Vijayarani, S. and Vinupriya, M., 2013. Performance analysis of Canny and Sobel edge detection algorithms in image mining. *International Journal of Innovative Research in Computer and Communication Engineering*, 1(8), pp. 1760–1767.

Vincent, O.R. and Folorunso, O., 2009, June. A descriptive algorithm for Sobel image edge detection. In *Proceedings of Informing Science & IT Education Conference (InSITE)* (Vol. 40, pp. 97–107). Informing Science Institute.

Ziou, D. and Tabbone, S., 1998. Edge detection techniques-an overview. *Pattern Recognition and Image Analysis C/C of Raspoznavaniye Obrazov I Analiz Izobrazhenii*, 8, pp. 537–559.

5

Frequency Domain Processing

Learning Objectives

After reading this chapter, the reader should have a clear understanding about:

- Low-pass filters/smoothing filters
- Ideal low-pass filters
- Butterworth low-pass filters
- Gaussian low-pass filters
- High-pass/sharpening filters
- Ideal high-pass filters
- Butterworth high-pass filters
- Gaussian high-pass filters

5.1 Introduction

In science or in control systems or in the image processing field, the term *frequency domain* is very important and is frequently employed. It means "analysis of the signals or functions" with respect to the frequency instead of "time". When the frequency domain is discussed, the next question could be: What is the difference between spatial and frequency domains? The answer is simple. In the spatial domain, the value of the pixels in an image normally changes with respect to the scene. It is "dealing with the image as it is". In the spatial domain, it means working on the intensity values of the image pixels. But, when it comes to the frequency domain, it is about transformation of the coefficient, instead of the direct manipulation of the pixels like in the spatial domain. To make the difference between the spatial domain and the frequency domain clearer, refer to Figure 5.1.

DOI: 10.1201/9781003217428-5

In other words, for the spatial domain:

1. It is about the manipulation or the processing of an input image, as it is to enhance the image for further operations or for the given application.
2. All the techniques that we know and discuss are about the direct operation or manipulation of the pixels in an image in the spatial domain.
3. The filters normally deployed are smoothing filters, edge detection filters, and sharpening filters.

The frequency domain can be explained with the help of the following points:

1. Here, the first step is all about conversion of an image from the spatial domain to frequency domain. Normally, one would use fast Fourier transform toward conversion of the spatial domain content to the frequency domain. (This is represented as "direct transformation" in Figure 5.1.)
2. Also, it is common practice to use low-pass filters for smoothing and high-pass filters for sharpening images ("frequency filter" in Figure 5.1).
3. After the processing is carried out up to this stage, the results available in hand are not ideal to be displayed as the output image. Hence, the inverse transformation is carried out to ensure the output image is accurately displayed.

Fourier transform is the real vital content in the entire process. This frequency domain analysis is normally carried out to understand how the signal energy gets distributed in a range of frequency.

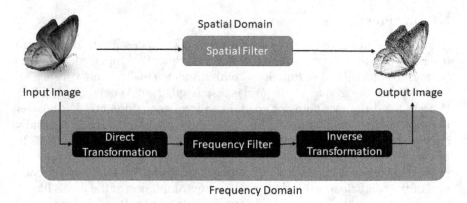

FIGURE 5.1
Spatial versus frequency domain.

5.2 Frequency Domain Flow

One should understand the complete flow of the frequency domain process.

Step 1: Use the fast Fourier transform to get the grayscale image into frequency transformation. (Here is where the input image gets transformed into frequency.) At the end of this step, one should get the spectrum available for further processing.

Step 2: The spectrum available might not be an easier choice to operate with the filters. Also, it is not an ideal choice for humans to visualize. Hence, there arises the need of further processing. Shifting the zero frequency component to the center of the spectrum is the step to be carried out.

Step 3: Apply the corresponding filters, such as low pass or high pass, based on the requirements to select/filter the frequencies.

Step 4: It is time for decentralization. One should get things back on track through this decentralization process.

Step 5: Apply the inverse fast Fourier transform, which enables conversion of the spectrum to a grayscale image, referred to as an output image. (Frequency to spatial transformation happens in the last step.)

The entire frequency domain process is presented as a diagrammatic representation in Figure 5.2. We will enhance this figure with the inclusion of the filters as this chapter progresses.

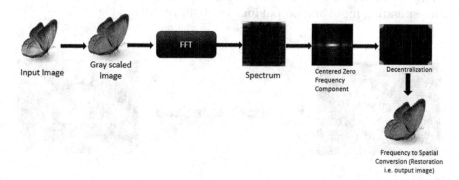

FIGURE 5.2
Frequency domain process.

5.3 Low-Pass Filters: A Deeper Dive

The purpose of the low-pass filter is to smooth or blur the image. The low-frequency contents will be retained, while attenuating the high-frequency contents. See Figure 5.3 for how a low-pass filter works.

The following sections discuss the types of low-pass filters.

5.3.1 Ideal Low-Pass Filter

The ideal low-pass filter, also known as the ILPF, is the most commonly used filter for image smoothing in the frequency domain. As expected, the ILPF removes the high-frequency content (noise) from the image and retains the low-frequency components.

One could mathematically represent the low-pass filter through the function

$$H(u,v) = \begin{cases} 1 & D(u,v) \leq D_0 \\ 0 & D(u,v) > D_0 \end{cases}$$

where D_0 is a positive constant and the filter retains all the frequency components within the radius D_0. All the frequency components outside the radius of the circle will be eliminated. In most cases, it will be the high-frequency components eliminated. Within the circle, the retention happens without attenuation. D_0 is referred to as the cut-off frequency.

$D(u, v)$ is the Euclidean distance from any point (u, v) to the origin of the frequency plane. Refer to Figure 5.4 to understand the impact of the D_0 value variations. Note that if the value of D_0 is very minimal, there is a risk of losing the core information and the image would be over blurred or smoothed. Hence, it is important to choose the apt D_0 value.

Figure 5.5 shows the earlier Figure 5.2 included with the ideal low-pass filter. The MATLAB code for the ideal low-pass filter is given next, and its corresponding input and output images are illustrated in Figure 5.6.

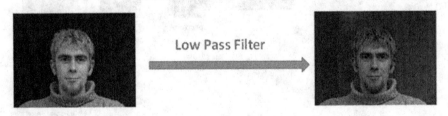

FIGURE 5.3
Low-pass filter results.

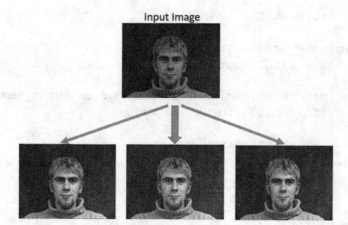

FIGURE 5.4
Ideal low-pass filter.

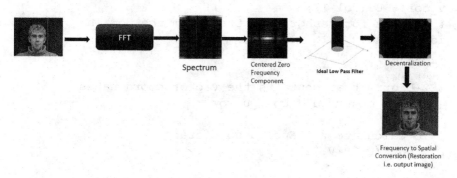

FIGURE 5.5
Ideal low-pass filter.

FIGURE 5.6
Ideal low-pass filter.

```
% Ideal Low Pass Filter coding

input_image = imread('test1.png');
[row, col] = size(input_image);

% To estimate the Fourier Transform of an input_image
FT_img = fft2(double(input_image));

% D0 is the Cut-off Frequency
D0 = 30;

% Filter Design
% Set the variables range
u_row = 0:(row-1);
% indices for meshgrid to transform the domain
index = find(u_row>row/2);
u_row(index) = u_row(index)-row;
% Set variables range
v_col = 0:(col-1);
% indices for meshgrid to transform the domain
idy = find(v_col>col/2);
v_col(idy) = v_col(idy)-col;

% 2-D grid that contains the vector coordinates
[V, U] = meshgrid(v_col, u_row);

% To calculate the Euclidean distance
D = sqrt(U.^2+V.^2);

% Filtering mask
H = double(D <= D0);

% Convolution
G = H.*FT_img;

% Resulting output image
output_image = real(ifft2(double(G)));

% To display input and output Images
subplot(2, 1, 1), imshow(input_image),
subplot(2, 1, 2), imshow(output_image, [ ]);
```

5.3.2 Butterworth Low-Pass Filter

Next up is the Butterworth low-pass filter (BLPF). It is interesting when you compare it with the ideal low-pass filter.

The Butterworth low-pass filter is something special. It is used to provide a frequency response as flat as possible. It is normally said to be used for image smoothing when it comes to the frequency domain. The Butterworth low-pass filter is very helpful in removal of high-frequency noise from the input image, while preserving the low-frequency contents.

The Butterworth filter's frequency response is to be noted. It has no sharp frequency response transition. When compared with the ideal low-pass filter, BLPF is said to have a very smooth transition.

The transition between the stop band and pass band is totally determined by the order of the filter. Here, we represent it with n. n determines the steepness of the transition between the bands. The transition could be soft and gentle, or it can as well be abrupt and sudden. So, based on the value of n, one can determine the transition. The ideal low-pass filter is said to have something called a ringing effect. It has to be avoided and the BLPF can overcome the ringing effect.

The transfer function of BLPF is presented as follows:

$$H(u,v) = \frac{1}{1 + \left[D(u,v)/D_0 \right]^{2n}}$$

where D_0 is termed the cut-off frequency and it is always regarded as the transition point between 1 and 0 ($H(u, v) = 1$ and $H(u, v) = 0$). The BLPF works based on the D_0 value. It passes all the frequencies inferior to D_0, whereas it cuts off all the frequencies above the D_0.

Here, the reader has to observe one more point. If the ILPF is considered, the transition could have been sharper, but when it is the BLPF, a smooth transition happens between 1 and 0. This is the reason the BLPF is said to fight ringing effects.

In the preceding function, n defines the order. The higher the order, the more it will look and behave similar to the ILPF. $D(u, v)$ is the Euclidean distance from any point (u, v) to the origin of the frequency plane. It is always important to know the distance of every element of the transfer function to the origin $(0,0)$.

Refer to Figure 5.7 to understand the process flow with the BLPF.

The MATLAB code for the Butterworth low-pass filter is given next, and its corresponding input and output images are illustrated in Figure 5.8.

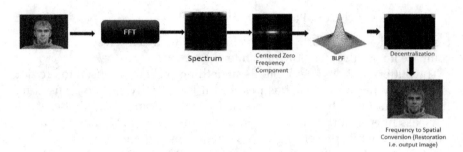

FIGURE 5.7
Butterworth low-pass filter.

FIGURE 5.8
Butterworth low-pass filter.

```
input_image = imread('test1.png');

[row, col] = size(input_image);

% To estimate the Fourier Transform of the input_image

FT_img = fft2(double(input_image));

% the order of "n" to be assigned
n = 2;

% Cut-off Frequency
D0 = 20;

% Filter Design
% Set the variables range
u_row = 0:(row-1);
% indices for meshgrid to transform the domain
index = find(u_row>row/2);
```

```
u_row(index) = u_row(index)-row;
% Set the variables range
v_col = 0:(col-1);
% indices for meshgrid to transform the domain
idy = find(v_col>col/2);
v_col(idy) = v_col(idy)-col;

% 2-D grid that contains the vector coordinates
[V, U] = meshgrid(v_col, u_row);

% To calculate the Euclidean distance
D = sqrt(U.^2 + V.^2);

% Filtering mask
H = 1./(1 + (D./D0).^(2*n));

% Convolution
G = H.*FT_img;

% Resulting output image obtained by applying Inverse
Fourier Transform of the convoluted image with the
MATLAB library function
% ifft2 - 2D inverse fast fourier transform

output_image = real(ifft2(double(G)));

% To display input and output images
subplot(2, 1, 1), imshow(input_image),
subplot(2, 1, 2), imshow(output_image, [ ]);
```

The next filter in queue to be discussed is the Gaussian low-pass filter.

5.3.3 Gaussian Low-Pass Filter

There are still some disadvantages with the BLPF. Yes, when the order is increased in the BLPF, one could still experience the ringing effect. The BLPF will start functioning like the ILPF and, hence, the ringing effect is unavoidable.

In order to overcome this, try the Gaussian filter. There is no ringing effect problem with the Gaussian filter. The most important point is there is "no consideration of the order of the filter". But, there is another new component to be included. It is σ, i.e., standard deviation. The σ also is very useful to measure the spread of the Gaussian curve.

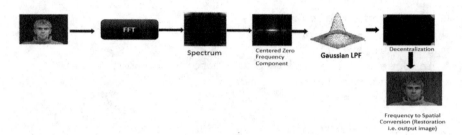

FIGURE 5.9
Gaussian low-pass filter.

The transfer function for the Gaussian low-pass filter is presented as follows:

$$H(u,v) = e^{\frac{-D^2(u,v)}{2D_0^2}}$$

where D_0 specifies the cut-off frequency as prompted by the user and $D(u, v)$ is the Euclidean distance from any point (u, v) to the origin of the frequency plane. It is important to know the distance of every element of the transfer function to the origin $(0,0)$.

Now let us to apply σ in place of D_0. If σ is assigned, then $H(u, v)$ becomes

$$H(u,v) = e^{-D^2(u,v)/2\sigma^2}$$

As mentioned earlier, σ is a measure for the spread of data. The process is presented pictorially in Figure 5.9.

The MATLAB code for the Gaussian low-pass filter is given next, and its corresponding input and output images and transfer function are illustrated in Figure 5.10.

```
input_image=double(imread('test1.png'));

FFT_img1=fft2(input_image);

figure(1),imshow(uint8(input_image))
figure(2),imagesc(log(1+abs(FFT_img1)))

[height,width]=size(input_image);
for x=1:1:height
  for y=1:1:width
    f(x,y)=input_image(x,y)*(-1)^(x+y);
  end
end
```

```
F=fft2(f);
figure(3),imagesc(log(1+abs(F)))

D0=35;
n=2;
for u=1:1:height
  for v=1:1:width
    D(u,v)=sqrt((u-height/2)^2+(v-width/2)^2);
    H(u,v)=exp(-((D(u,v)*D(u,v))/(2*D0*D0)));
  end
end

figure(4), imshow(H)
figure(5), mesh(H)

G=F.*H;
g=abs(ifft2(G));
figure(6), imshow(uint8(g))
```

Table 5.1 compares the aforementioned low-pass filters.

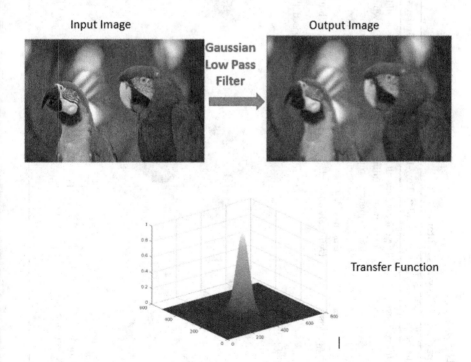

FIGURE 5.10
Gaussian low-pass filter.

TABLE 5.1

Comparison of Low-Pass Filters

Parameter	Ideal Low-Pass Filter	Butterworth Low-Pass Filter	Gaussian Low-Pass Filter
Cut-off frequency, D_0	The filter retains all the frequency components within the radius D_0. All the frequency components outside the radius of the circle are eliminated.	It passes all the frequencies inferior to the D_0, whereas it cuts off all the frequencies above the D_0. The transition is smooth.	The transition is much smoother because of inclusion of σ.
Ringing effects	Definitely affected.	Affected, but not as much as with the ideal low-pass filter. When the order is increased, the ringing effect appears.	Totally eliminated due to inclusion of σ. σ is a measure for the spread of data.
Transfer function			
Filter view			
Mathematical representation	$H(u,v) = \begin{cases} 1 & D(u,v) \le D_0 \\ 0 & D(u,v) > D_0 \end{cases}$	$H(u,v) = \dfrac{1}{1 + \left[D(u,v)/D_0 \right]^{2n}}$	$H(u,v) = e^{\frac{-D^2(u,v)}{2D_0^2}}$

5.4 High-Pass Filters/Sharpening Filters

The next topic of discussion is the high-pass filter and its functionalities. A high-pass filter enables passing of high frequencies while managing to suppress the low frequencies. It is also referred to as a sharpening filter, as it does sharpening in the frequency domain. For a visual of the sharpening process, see Figure 5.11. There are multiple variants of the high-pass filter available for usage. They are the ideal high-pass filter, Butterworth high-pass filter, and Gaussian high-pass filter, the same nomenclature as low-pass filters. All three will be covered next with clear and concise explanations.

5.4.1 Ideal High-Pass Filter

The ideal high-pass filter (IHPF) is one of the filters used for the image sharpening process and the same was conveyed a little earlier in the previous section. Image sharpening is carried out in order to enhance the "fine, sharp" details in the image and to clearly highlight the edges in a digital image. As the name suggests, the IHPF clearly removes and suppresses the low-frequency components while retaining the high-frequency components. Since we have learned the functioning of the ILPF, one can expect the reverse of it with the IHPF.

The transfer function for the ideal high-pass filter can be presented as

$$H(u,v) = \begin{cases} 0 & D(u,v) \leq D_0 \\ 1 & D(u,v) > D_0 \end{cases}$$

where D_0 is the positive constant. The filter retains all the frequency components outside the radius D_0. All the frequency components inside the radius of the circle are suppressed. In most cases it will be all the low-frequency components getting suppressed.

The next important term to know is the cut-off frequency. D_0 is the transition point between $H(u, v) = 1$ and $H(u, v) = 0$, and hence it becomes the cut-off frequency.

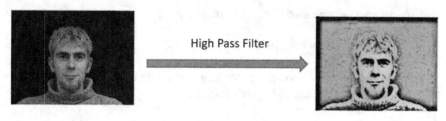

FIGURE 5.11
Sharpened image.

Also from the equation, D(u, v) is the Euclidean distance from any point (u, v) to the origin of the frequency plane.

Refer to Figure 5.12 to understand how the ideal high-pass filter works.

The MATLAB code for the ideal high-pass filter is given next, and its corresponding input and output images are illustrated in Figure 5.13.

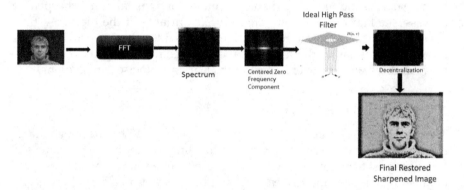

FIGURE 5.12
Ideal high-pass filter process.

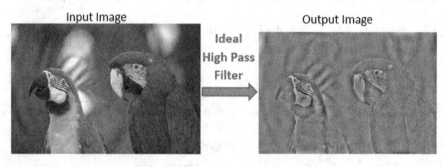

FIGURE 5.13
Ideal high-pass filter.

```
% Ideal High Pass Filter

input_image = imread('test1.png');

[row, col] = size(input_image);

% To estimate the Fourier Transform of the input_image
FT_img = fft2(double(input_image));

% Cut-off frequency
D0 = 10;
```

```
% Filter Design
% Set the variables range
u_row = 0:(row-1);
% indices for meshgrid to transform the domain
index = find(u_row>row/2);
u_row(index) = u_row(index)-row;
% Set the variables range
v_col = 0:(col-1);
% indices for meshgrid to transform the domain
idy = find(v_col>col/2);
v_col(idy) = v_col(idy)-col;

% meshgrid (v, u) returns 2-D grid coordinates contained
in the specified vectors v and u
[V, U] = meshgrid(v_col, u_row);

% To calculate the Euclidean distance
D = sqrt(U.^2+V.^2);

% Filtering mask
H = double(D > D0);

% Convolution
G = H.*FT_img;

% Resulting output image
output_image = real(ifft2(double(G)));
% To display input and output images
subplot(2, 1, 1), imshow(input_image),
subplot(2, 1, 2), imshow(output_image, [ ]);
```

The next topic to be discussed is the Butterworth high-pass filter.

5.4.2 Butterworth High-Pass Filter

The Butterworth high-pass filter (BHPF) is used for image sharpening like any other high-pass filter. However, the BHPF preserves the high-frequency components, while suppressing the low-frequency ones.

Following is the transfer function for the BHPF:

$$H(u,v) = \frac{1}{1+\left[D_0/D(u,v)\right]^{2n}}$$

where D_0 is termed the cut-off frequency and is the transition point between 1 and 0 ($H(u, v) = 1$ and $H(u, v) = 0$); n defines the order; and $D(u, v)$ is the

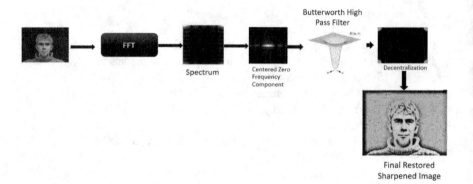

FIGURE 5.14
Butterworth high-pass filter process.

FIGURE 5.15
Butterworth high-pass filter.

Euclidean distance from any point (u, v) to the origin of the frequency plane. The BHPF works based on the D_0 value. It passes all the frequencies above D_0, whereas it suppresses all the frequencies below D_0. A Butterworth high-pass filter keeps frequencies outside radius D_0 and discards values inside.

See Figure 5.14 for a diagram of the BHPF process.

The MATLAB code for the Butterworth high-pass filter is given next, and its corresponding input and output images are illustrated in Figure 5.15.

```
% Butterworth High Pass Filter

input_image = imread('test1.png');

[row, col] = size(input_image);

% To estimate the Fourier Transform of the input_image
with MATLAB library function fft2 (2-D fast fourier
transform)
FT_img = fft2(double(input_image));
```

```
% Order of n
n = 2;

% Cut-off Frequency
D0 = 10;
% Filter Design
% Set the variables range
u_row = 0:(row-1);
% indices for meshgrid to transform the domain
index = find(u_row>row/2);
u_row(index) = u_row(index)-row;
% Set the variables range
v_col = 0:(col-1);
% indices for meshgrid to transform the domain
idy = find(v_col>col/2);
v_col(idy) = v_col(idy)-col;

% 2-D grid that contains the vector coordinates
[V, U] = meshgrid(v_col, u_row);

% Euclidean distance
D = sqrt(U.^2 + V.^2);

% Filtering mask
H = 1./(1 + (D0./D).^(2*n));

% Convolution
G = H.*FT_img;

% Resulting output image
output_image = real(ifft2(double(G)));

% To display input and output images
subplot(2, 1, 1), imshow(input_image),
subplot(2, 1, 2), imshow(output_image, [ ]);
```

The next filter to be explained is the Gaussian high-pass filter.

5.4.3 Gaussian High-Pass Filter

The Gaussian high-pass filter has the same ideology as the ideal and Butterworth high-pass filters. But there is an important aspect to be understood. The transitions are much smoother than the previous two. The transfer function is presented as follows:

$$H(u,v) = 1 - e^{-D^2(u,v)/2D_0^2}$$

where D_0 specifies the cut-off frequency as prompted by the user and $D(u, v)$ is the Euclidean distance from any point (u, v) to the origin of the frequency plane.

Refer to Figure 5.16 to understand the Gaussian high-pass filter. The MATLAB code for the Gaussian high-pass filter is given next, and its corresponding input and output images and transfer function are illustrated in Figure 5.17.

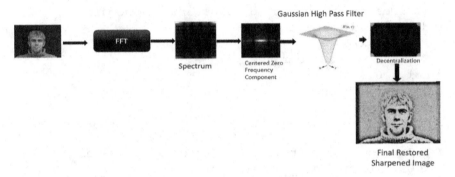

FIGURE 5.16
The Gaussian high-pass filter process.

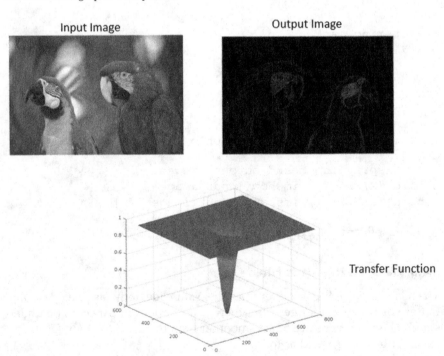

FIGURE 5.17
Gaussian high-pass filter.

```
% Gaussian High Pass Filter

input_image=double(imread('test1.png'));
FT_img=fft2(input_image);

figure(1),imshow(uint8(input_image))
figure(2),imagesc(log(1+abs(FT_img)))

[height,width]=size(input_image);
for x=1:1:height
  for y=1:1:width
    f(x,y)=input_image(x,y)*(-1)^(x+y);
  end
end

F=fft2(f);
figure(3),imagesc(log(1+abs(F)))

D0=35;
n=2;
for u=1:1:height
  for v=1:1:width
    D(u,v)=sqrt((u-height/2)^2+(v-width/2)^2);
    H(u,v)=1-(exp(-((D(u,v)*D(u,v))/(2*D0*D0)))));
  end
end

figure(4), imshow(H)
figure(5), mesh(H)

G=F.*H;
g=abs(ifft2(G));
figure(6), imshow(uint8(g))
```

See Table 5.2 for a comparison of high-pass filters, and Table 5.3 for a comparison of low-pas filters versus high-pass filters.

The significance of frequency domain has been explored in this chapter. The next chapter explores image segmentation, its associated algorithms, and the processes of dilation and erosion.

TABLE 5.2

Comparison of High-Pass Filters

Parameter	Ideal High-Pass Filter	Butterworth High-Pass Filter	Gaussian High-Pass Filter
Cut-off frequency, D_0	The filter retains all the frequency components outside the radius D_0. All the frequency components inside the radius of the circle are suppressed.	It works based on the D_0 value. It passes all the frequencies above the D_0 whereas it suppresses all the frequencies below the D_0. A Butterworth high-pass filter keeps frequencies outside the radius D_0 and discards values inside.	The transition is much smoother compared to the other two filters.
Transfer function			
Filter view			
Mathematical representation	$H(u,v) = \begin{cases} 0 & D(u,v) \leq D_0 \\ 1 & D(u,v) > D_0 \end{cases}$	$H(u,v) = \dfrac{1}{1 + \left[D_0 / D(u,v) \right]^{2n}}$	$H(u,v) = 1 - e^{-D^2(u,v)/2D_0^2}$

TABLE 5.3

Low-Pass Filters versus High-Pass Filters

Low-Pass Filter	High-Pass Filter
The low-pass filter is mainly meant for smoothing an image.	A high-pass filter is meant for sharpening an image.
It accepts/allows only the low-frequency components, diminishing the high-frequency ones.	It accepts/allows only the high-frequency components, diminishing the low-frequency ones.
The low-pass filter allows the frequency components that are below the cut-off frequency to pass through it.	The high-pass filter allows the frequencies above the cut-off frequency to pass through it.

5.5 Quiz

1. Which of the following is not a filter type?
   a. Ideal low-pass filter
   b. Ideal high-pass filter
   c. Butterworth low-pass filter
   d. Gaussian medium-pass filter

2. Which of the following provides no ringing effect?
   a. Gaussian low-pass filter
   b. Ideal low-pass filter
   c. Butterworth low-pass filter
   d. None of the above

3. Which of the following are mainly meant for smoothing an image?
   a. Low-pass filters
   b. High-pass filters
   c. All of the above
   d. None of the above

4. High-pass filters allow only low-frequency components, diminishing the high-frequency ones. True or false?

5. _____ accept/allow only high-frequency components, diminishing the low-frequency ones.

6. Which of the following statements is false?
   a. Low-pass filters allow frequency components that are below the cut-off frequency to pass through.

b. High-pass filters allow frequencies above the cut-off frequency to pass through.

c. High-pass filters are mainly meant for smoothing an image.

5.5.1 Answers

1. d
2. a
3. a
4. False
5. High-pass filters
6. c

5.6 Review Questions

1. What is a low-pass filter all about?
2. What are the types of low-pass filters mentioned in this chapter?
3. Explain the transfer function of the ideal low-pass filter.
4. How is the ideal low-pass filter different from the Butterworth low-pass filter?
5. Which of the low-pass filters is the best to fight ringing effect?
6. How does a high-pass filter work?
7. How many types of high-pass filters are generally used?
8. What are the major differences between low-pass and high-pass filters?

5.6.1 Answers

1. A low-pass filter is mainly meant for smoothing an image. It accepts/allows only the low-frequency components, diminishing the high-frequency ones.
2. The three types are ideal low-pass filter, Butterworth low-pass filter, and Gaussian low-pass filter.
3. One could mathematically represent the low-pass filter through the function

$$H(u,v) = \begin{cases} 1 & D(u,v) \le D_0 \\ 0 & D(u,v) > D_0 \end{cases}$$

From this equation, D_0 is the positive constant. The filter retains all the frequency components within the radius D_0. All the frequency components outside the radius of the circle are eliminated. In most cases it all the high-frequency components eliminated. Within the circle, the retention happens without attenuation. D_0 is also referred to as the cut-off frequency.

Also, D(u, v) is the Euclidean distance from any point (u, v) to the origin of the frequency plane. Note that if the value of D_0 is very minimal, there is a risk of losing the core information, and it would be over blurred or smoothed. Hence, it is important to choose the apt D_0 value.

4. The ideal low-pass filter retains all the frequency components within the radius D_0. All the frequency components outside the radius of the circle are eliminated. The Butterworth low-pass filter passes all the frequencies inferior to the D_0, whereas it cuts off all the frequencies above the D_0. The transition is smoothed with the Butterworth filter.

5. Gaussian low-pass filter.

6. It accepts/allows only the high-frequency components, diminishing the low-frequency ones.

7. There are three types: ideal high-pass filter, Butterworth high-pass filter, and Gaussian high-pass filter.

8. See Table 5.3.

Further Reading

Burt, P.J., 1981. Fast filter transform for image processing. *Computer Graphics and Image Processing*, 16(1), pp. 20–51.

Chen, C.F., Zhu, C.R. and Song, H.Q., 2007. Image enhancement based on Butterworth low-pass filter [J]. *Modern Electronics Technique*, 30(24), pp. 163–168.

Dogra, A. and Bhalla, P., 2014. Image sharpening by gaussian and Butterworth high-pass filter. *Biomedical and Pharmacology Journal*, 7(2), pp. 707–713.

Dogra, A. and Bhalla, P., 2014. Image sharpening by gaussian and Butterworth high-pass filter. *Biomedical and Pharmacology Journal*, 7(2), pp. 707–713.

Govind, D., Ginley, B., Lutnick, B., Tomaszewski, J.E. and Sarder, P., 2018. Glomerular detection and segmentation from multimodal microscopy images using a Butterworth band-pass filter. In *Medical imaging 2018: Digital pathology* (Vol. 10581, p. 1058114). International Society for Optics and Photonics.

Khorsheed, O.K., 2014. Produce low-pass and high-pass image filter in java. *International Journal of Advances in Engineering & Technology*, 7(3), p. 712.

Toet, A., 1989. Image fusion by a ratio of low-pass pyramid. *Pattern Recognition Letters*, 9(4), pp. 245–253.

Zhang, Z. and Zhao, G., 2011, July. Butterworth filter and Sobel edge detection to image. In *2011 International Conference on Multimedia Technology* (pp. 254–256). IEEE.

6

Image Segmentation: A Clear Analysis and Understanding

Learning Objectives

After reading this chapter, the reader should have a clear understanding about:

- Image segmentation
- Why segmentation is important?
- Image segmentation algorithms
- Thresholding-based image segmentation
- Segmentation algorithms based on edge information
- Segmentation algorithms based on region information
- Segmentation algorithms based on the clustering approach
- Morphological segmentation
- Texture-based segmentation

6.1 Introduction

Let us first understand what segmentation is all about. Let us start with an example. In Figure 6.1 we have only one object: a motorcycle. It is very straightforward for the algorithms to predict the content in the given image. But, there comes a challenge when we have a car and motorcycle together in a single image, as presented in Figure 6.2. Here in this case, we need our algorithm to clearly identify the location of the objects and to go ahead with object detection of the car and motorcycle from the image. Now comes the segmentation of the picture. Before even going ahead with the classification, one would need to clearly understand what the image consists of, i.e., what is

DOI: 10.1201/9781003217428-6

FIGURE 6.1
One object.

FIGURE 6.2
Two objects.

the content of the image, and this can be achieved through image segmentation (Figure 6.3).

It is time to further define image segmentation in an "image processing way". *Image segmentation* is a process or a technique of partitioning a given image into multiple subgroups based on common properties, such as intensity or texture. The process groups together pixels of similar properties, thereby identifying the image's objects. Through this approach of dividing into multiple subgroups, analyzing the image becomes much easier and effective, while also reducing the complexity to a greater extent.

FIGURE 6.3
Object detection.

Image segmentation is one of the most crucial and challenging tasks in image processing and computer vision. It is crucial because the outcome of the entire analysis of an image is dictated by the quality of output from the segmentation stage since all further analysis measurements are based on the measurements done on these segmented regions. If proper segmentation is carried out, then the results will be of high accuracy.

Segmentation is challenging because of the variability in the shapes of the objects of interest and the variability in the quality of the input image. The quality of input image may be poor due to multiple factors such as nonuniform lighting, shadows, noise, existence of overlap among objects, and poor contrast between objects and background.

The goal of image segmentation is twofold:

1. To separate different regions in an image (e.g., car and motorcycle).

2. To separate a specific region of interest (e.g., car or motorcycle) from the image. In the continuum from image processing to computer vision, image segmentation is a midlevel process. The input to the midlevel process is an image and the output is the attributes extracted from the image. The midlevel process consists of image segmentation, representation, and description. Image segmentation consists of partitioning an image into its constituent nonoverlapping regions. Once the image has been segmented, the resulting individual regions (or objects) can be represented, described, analyzed, and classified. An example of segmentation is given in Figure 6.4.

 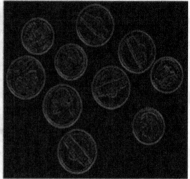

FIGURE 6.4
After segmentation.

6.2 Types of Segmentation

There are many types of segmentation techniques available and one can choose the best fit for the process. The segmentation types discussed here are thresholding, histogram-based, region-based, edge-based, clustering-based, morphological transforms, and texture-based.

First we will briefly introduce each technique, and the remaining sections of the chapter will go into depth for each technique.

a. Thresholding method.

   Segmentation algorithms based on a thresholding approach are suitable for images where there is a distinct difference between object and background. The goal of thresholding-based segmentation algorithms is to divide an image into two distinct regions – object and background – directly based on intensity values and/or properties of these values. Thresholding is viewed as one of the simplest techniques for image segmentation. There are three types of thresholding-based image segmentation followed. They are:

   - Global thresholding
   - Variable thresholding
   - Multiple thresholding

b. Histogram-based segmentation.

   A histogram of an image is a plot between intensity levels (i.e., gray levels) along the x-axis and the number (frequency) of pixels at each gray level along the y-axis. A good threshold can be found from the histogram if the histogram peak is tall, narrow, symmetric, and separated by deep valleys, and based on this the foreground and the background can be separated.

c. Region-based segmentation.

The region-based segmentation method segments the image into various regions of similar characteristics. A region is a group of connected pixels with similar properties. There are two techniques that fall under this segmentation and they are region growing, and region split and merge.

d. Edge-based segmentation.

Edges are defined as "sudden and significant changes in the intensity" of an image. These changes happen between the boundaries of an object in an image. The edges are detected based on the significant change in intensity between the objects in the image. So, in an image, if there are many objects, edges are the easiest way to identify all of them. If the segmentation is carried out based on the edges, we can classify it as edge-based segmentation. Based on the discontinuity or dissimilarities, edge-based segmentation will be carried out. It is unlike region-based segmentation, which is completely based on similarity.

e. Clustering-based segmentation.

Clustering-based techniques segment the image into clusters having pixels with similar characteristics. There are many types of clustering techniques available, but we will learn of the ones that have a proven success rate in image processing.

f. Morphological transforms-based segmentation.

Morphology is the study of shapes. Morphological image processing refers to a set of image processing operations that process images based on shapes and not on pixel intensities. If the segmentation if carried out based on the shapes, we refer to it as morphological transforms-based segmentation.

g. Texture-based segmentation approaches.

Segmentation based on texture characteristics consists of dividing an image into different regions based on similarity in texture features. Texture is defined as a repeated pattern of information or arrangement of the structure with regular intervals. The texture of images refers to the appearance, structure, and arrangement of the parts of an object within the image.

We will now go in depth into all the aforementioned techniques.

6.3 Thresholding Method

As discussed in brief, segmentation algorithms based on the thresholding approach are suitable for images where there is a distinct difference between the object and background. The goal of thresholding-based segmentation algorithms is to divide an image into two distinct regions – object and background – directly based on intensity values and/or properties of these values. This is viewed as one of the simplest techniques for image segmentation. Let us understand things in detail.

There is an important component called threshold involved, and based on the threshold T, one could go ahead with the following types of thresholding-based segmentation algorithms:

- Segmentation algorithm based on a global threshold
- Segmentation algorithm based on multiple thresholds
- Segmentation based on the histogram for thresholding
- Segmentation algorithm based on a variable threshold

6.3.1 Segmentation Algorithm Based on a Global Threshold

When the intensity distribution of object and background pixels in an image are sufficiently distinct, segmentation can be done by using a single global threshold over the entire image.

Consider an image $f(x,y)$ with light objects on a dark background. To extract objects from the image, select a threshold T. A pixel in an image is considered as part of the object if the pixel intensity is greater than threshold T. Similarly, if the pixel intensity is less than or equal to threshold T, then that pixel is considered as the background component. Mathematically, this can be expressed as

$$g(x,y) = \begin{cases} 1 \text{ if } f(x,y) > T \\ 0 \text{ if } f(x,y) \leq T \end{cases} \tag{6.1}$$

where g(x,y) represents the output image (segmented image), f(x,y) represents the input image, and T represents the threshold.

6.3.1.1 Selection of Optimal Global Threshold Using a Basic Iterative Algorithm

Finding an optimal global threshold through an iterative algorithm will work well when there is a clear valley between the modes of the histogram related to objects and the background. The basic iterative algorithm for finding the global threshold T is as follows:

1. Select an initial estimate for the global threshold T.
2. Segment the image by using the following approach, which was detailed earlier:

$$g(x,y) = \begin{cases} G1 \text{ if } f(x,y) > T \\ G2 \text{ if } f(x,y) \leq T \end{cases} \qquad (6.2)$$

where G1 and G2 are groups 1 and 2, respectively. G1 is pixels with intensity values >T and G2 is pixels with intensity values ≤T.

3. Compute m_1 and m_2:

   m_1 = average of intensity values of pixels within G_1.

   m_2 = average of intensity values of pixels within G_2.

4. Compute a new threshold value: $T = \dfrac{m_1 + m_2}{2}$.
5. Repeat step 2 to step 5 until the difference between T in successive iterations is less than the specified ΔT.

This algorithm is an iterative scheme for finding the optimal global threshold, and parameter ΔT is used as a stopping criterion, i.e., when the difference in threshold between two successive iterations becomes less than ΔT (say, ΔT = 0.05), the algorithm stops iterating and it is said to have converged to the optimum solution, i.e., the optimum global threshold.

6.3.1.2 Selection of Global Threshold Using Otsu Method

Otsu thresholding uses an image histogram to find the optimal global threshold.

Goal: To find an optimal global threshold. The optimal global threshold is the one that minimizes the weighted within-class (intraclass) variance. Minimizing the weighted within-class variance is the same as maximizing the between-class (interclass) variance. The Otsu method finds an optimum global threshold that maximizes the interclass variance. Interclass variance should be maximized for the following reasons:

- The threshold classes should be distinct.
- There should be best separation between classes.

Assumptions:

- The histogram of the image is bimodal.
- Uniform illumination (implicitly) is assumed, so the bimodal brightness behavior arises only from object appearance differences.

Algorithm

Step 1: Normalize the image histogram.

Consider a grayscale image with L gray levels. The grayscale intensities in this image ranges from 0 to $L-1$. The number of pixels at level i is denoted by n_i and the total number of pixels in an image is given by $N = \sum_{i=0}^{L-1} n_i$. The histogram of the image is normalized and this normalized histogram is considered as probability distribution, given by Equation 6.3:

$$p_i = \frac{n_i}{N} \tag{6.3}$$

where $p_i > 0$ and $\sum_{i=0}^{L-1} p_i = 1$.

Step 2: Find the cumulative sum.

Select a threshold: $T(k) = k$, where $0 < k < L-1$.

Dichotomize the pixels in the grayscale image into classes C_1 and C_2 using this threshold k. C_1 is all pixels with intensity from 0 to k. C_2 is all pixels with intensity from $k+1$ to $L-1$.

The probability of occurrence of class C_1 and class C_2 is given by Equation 6.4 and Equation 6.5, respectively:

$$P(C_1) = P_1(k) = \sum_{i=0}^{k} p_i \tag{6.4}$$

$$P(C_2) = P_2(k) = \sum_{i=k+1}^{L-1} p_i = 1 - P_1(k) \tag{6.5}$$

Step 3: Find the cumulative mean and global mean.

The mean intensity value of pixels within class C_1 is given by

$$m_1(k) = \sum_{i=0}^{k} i P(i|C_1) \tag{6.6}$$

From Bayes theorem,

$$P(i|C_1) = \frac{P(C_1|i)P(i)}{P(C_1)} \qquad (6.7)$$

where $P(i|C_1)$ is the probability of intensity value i, given that i comes from class C_1; $P(C_1|i)$ is the probability of C_1 given i; $P(i)$ is the probability of the ith value, which is the ith component of histogram p_i. Here, $P(C_1|i) = 1$, since we are dealing only with values of i from class C_1. Substituting $P(i)$ and $P(C_1|i)$ in Equation 6.7 becomes

$$P(i|C_1) = \frac{p_i}{P_1(k)} \left(\because P(i) = p_i \text{ and } P(C_1) = P_1(k) \text{ from } (6.4) \right) \qquad (6.8)$$

Substituting Equation 6.8 in Equation 6.6:

$$m_1(k) = \frac{1}{P_1(k)} \sum_{i=0}^{k} i\,p_i \qquad (6.9)$$

Similarly, the mean intensity values of pixels within class C_2 are given by

$$m_2(k) = \sum_{i=k+1}^{L-1} i\,P(i|C_2) \qquad (6.10)$$

$$m_2(k) = \frac{1}{P_2(k)} \sum_{i=k+1}^{L-1} i\,p_i \qquad (6.11)$$

The cumulative mean (average intensity) up to level k is given by

$$m(k) = \sum_{i=0}^{k} i\,p_i \qquad (6.12)$$

The average intensity of the entire image (global mean) is given by

$$m_G = \sum_{i=0}^{L-1} i\,p_i \qquad (6.13)$$

The relationships in Equations 6.14 and 6.15 hold for P_1, P_2, m_1 and m_2.

$$P_1 m_1 + P_2 m_2 = m_G \qquad (6.14)$$

$$P_1 + P_2 = 1 \qquad (6.15)$$

Step 4: Find the global variance and between-class variance.

In order to evaluate the effectiveness of threshold k, a dimensionless metric η is used:

$$\eta = \frac{\sigma_B^2}{\sigma_G^2} \tag{6.16}$$

where σ_B^2 is the between-class variance and σ_G^2 is the global variance, i.e., the intensity variance of all the pixels in the given image.

Global variance σ_G^2 is given by

$$\sigma_G^2 = \sum_{i=0}^{L-1} (i - m_G)^2 p_i \tag{6.17}$$

Between-class variance σ_B^2 is given by

$$\sigma_B^2 = P_1 (m_1 - m_G)^2 + P_2 (m_2 - m_G)^2 \tag{6.18}$$

where P_1 and P_2 are $P_1(k)$ and $P_2(k)$, respectively.

Equation 6.18 can also be written as

$$\sigma_B^2 = P_1 P_2 (m_1 - m_2)^2 \tag{6.19}$$

$$\sigma_B^2 = \frac{(P_1 m_G - m)^2}{P_1 (1 - P_1)} \tag{6.20}$$

Reintroducing k, we have

$$\eta(k) = \frac{\sigma_B^2(k)}{\sigma_G^2} \tag{6.21}$$

$$\sigma_B^2(k) = \frac{(P_1(k) m_G - m(k))^2}{P_1(k)(1 - P_1(k))} \tag{6.22}$$

Step 5: Find the optimum global threshold k^*.

The optimum global threshold value k^* is the one that maximizes Equation 6.23:

$$\sigma_B^2(k^*) = \max_{0 \le k \le L-1} \sigma_B^2(k) \tag{6.23}$$

To find k^*, evaluate Equation 6.23 for all integer values of k (subject to condition $0 < P_1(k) < 1$) and select the value of k that yields the maximum $\sigma_B^2(k)$. If $\sigma_B^2(k)$ is maximum for more than one value of k, average various values of k for which $\sigma_B^2(k)$ is maximum.

Step 6: Segment the input image using the optimum global threshold k^*.

Once k^* is obtained, the input image is segmented as follows:

$$g(x,y) = \begin{cases} 1 \text{ if } f(x,y) > k^* \\ 0 \text{ if } f(x,y) \leq k^* \end{cases} \quad (6.24)$$

Step 7: Estimation of separability of classes.

In order to evaluate the effectiveness of threshold k, a dimensionless metric η is used. The formula for σ_B^2 and σ_G^2 is discussed in step 4. Evaluate η at optimum global threshold k^*, i.e., find $\eta(k^*)$ to estimate the separability of classes.

In summary, to find the optimum global threshold using the Otsu algorithm:

1. Compute the normalized histogram of the input image. Denote the components of the histogram with p_i, where $i = 0,1,2,\ldots\ldots,L-1$.
2. Compute the cumulative sums $P_1(k)$ and $P_2(k)$ using Equation 6.3 and Equation 6.4, respectively.
3. Compute the cumulative mean $m(k)$ using Equation 6.12.
4. Compute the global intensity mean m_G using Equation 6.13.
5. Obtain the Otsu threshold k^* using Equation 6.23.
6. Obtain the separability measure $\eta *$ by evaluating Equation 6.21 at $k = k^*$.

Figure 6.5a shows the input image, which is an optical microscope image of polymersome cells. These are the cells that are artificially engineered using polymers. These cells are invisible to the human immune system and can be used for targeted drug delivery. Figure 6.5b shows the histogram of the input image. The goal is to segment the molecules from the background. Figure 6.5c shows the segmentation results obtained by using the basic iterative algorithm for global threshold. Since the histogram has no distinct valleys and since there is no distinct intensity difference between the object and background, this algorithm failed to produce the desired segmentation result. Figure 6.5d shows the segmentation result obtained by using Otsu's global threshold method. The results obtained by using Otsu's method is superior to the results obtained by using the iterative algorithm for global threshold. The threshold computed by using the basic iterative algorithm was 169, whereas the threshold computed by using Otsu's method was 182, which is closer to the lighter areas defining the cells in the input image. The separability measure obtained was $\eta * = 0.467$.

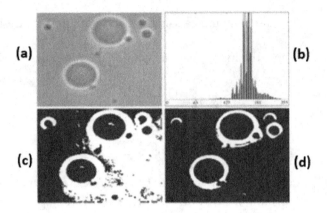

FIGURE 6.5
Global thresholding.

6.3.2 Segmentation Algorithm Based on Multiple Thresholds

Multiple thresholding is used when there are two light objects on a dark background in an image. Consider an image $f(x,y)$ with two light objects – object 1 with intensity a and object 2 with intensity b – and a dark background with intensity c.

To extract these two objects, consider two thresholds T_1 and T_2. Let T_1 denote the threshold for object 1 and let T_2 denote the threshold for object 2. A pixel is said to belong to object 1 if its intensity is greater than T_1 and less than or equal to T_2. A pixel is said to belong to object 2 if its intensity is greater than T_2. A pixel is said to belong to the background if its intensity is less than T_1. The segmented image is mathematically expressed as

$$g(x,y) = \begin{cases} a & \text{if } T_1 < f(x,y) \leq T_2 \\ b & \text{if } f(x,y) > T_2 \\ c & \text{if } f(x,y) \leq T_1 \end{cases} \qquad (6.25)$$

Here $g(x,y)$ denotes the segmented image, a denotes intensities of object 1, b denotes intensities of object 2, and c denotes the intensity of the background. T_1 denotes the threshold for object 1 and T_2 denotes the threshold for object 2.

6.4 Histogram-Based Segmentation

There are many techniques or methods followed for choosing the threshold value. One could make it a really simple option by choosing the threshold value manually. Or one can use a thresholding algorithm to compute what

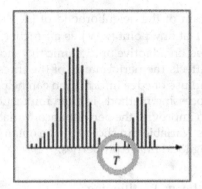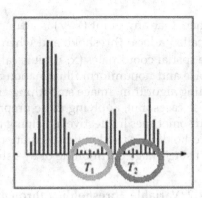

FIGURE 6.6
Single threshold and multiple threshold based on histogram.

the value could be. This approach is referred to as automatic thresholding. A very orderly and easy approach to automatic thresholding would be to use the mean value as the threshold. This is believed to be a very sensible approach for a technical reason. If the pixels are brighter than the background, they should certainly be brighter than the average.

There is another approach for identifying the threshold value. It is to create a histogram and use the valley point (as shown in the Figure 6.6) as the threshold value. Here, again to reiterate, the histogram is used to identify the threshold value.

The histogram of an image is the plot between intensity levels, i.e., gray levels, along the x-axis and the number of pixels at each gray level along the y-axis. Figure 6.6 shows selection of the threshold based on the image histogram. A good threshold can be found from the histogram if the histogram peak is tall, narrow, symmetric, and separated by deep valleys. A good threshold is the intensity value that is chosen from the bottom of the valley of the histogram.

The left-hand side of Figure 6.6 has the histogram of an image with a single object on a dark background. A single threshold T is chosen from valleys of the histogram to segment this single light object from the dark background. The right-hand side of Figure 6.6 has the histogram of two light objects on a dark background. In this case, two thresholds T_1 and T_2 are used to segment these two light objects from the dark background. In the histogram of Figure 6.6, the horizontal axis (x-axis) denotes the gray levels and the vertical axis (y-axis) denotes the number of pixels at each gray level.

6.4.1 Segmentation Algorithm Based on a Variable Threshold

When the threshold T changes over the image, it is called a variable threshold. This variable threshold value at point (x, y) can be selected either based on the neighborhood of (x, y) or based on the spatial coordinates (x, y).

When T at any point (x, y) is a function of the neighborhood of (x, y), it is called a local threshold, and when T at any point (x, y) is a function of the spatial coordinates (x, y), it is called an adaptive or dynamic threshold. Noise and nonuniform illumination affects the performance of the thresholding algorithm. Image smoothing and use of edge information can help in these cases. But, applying these preprocessing methods is often impractical and sometimes ineffective in helping to improvise the performance. Variable thresholding is used in these situations. Variable thresholds can be obtained by using image partitioning or by using local image properties.

6.4.2 Variable Thresholding through Image Partitioning

Logic: Partition an image into nonoverlapping rectangles and apply any one of the thresholding algorithms as required for each subimage individually.

Figure 6.7 has, first, the input image. Then, the image is subdivided into nonoverlapping regions, i.e., the input image is divided into six nonoverlapping

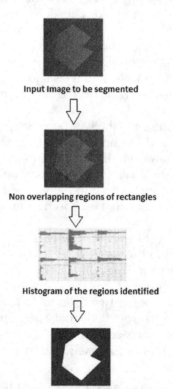

Input Image to be segmented

Non overlapping regions of rectangles

Histogram of the regions identified

Segmented result with local thresholding
(Can choose any other thresholding method)

FIGURE 6.7
Segmentation based on variable thresholding.

rectangles. The histogram for those regions is found next, and then the segmentation based on the local thresholding method is applied to arrive at the final segmented image.

6.5 Region-Based Segmentation

Region-based segmentation methods segment the image into various regions of similar characteristics. A region is a group of connected pixels with similar properties. There are two techniques that fall under this segmentation: (1) region growing and (2) region split and merge.

We will introduce the region-growing technique first.

6.5.1 Region-Growing Method

The goal of the region-growing method is to group the pixels or subregions into larger regions based on predefined criteria. This is considered as the simplest of the techniques and it starts with the seed points. From the seed points, the growth happens. The growth is governed by appending to each seed point those of nearby or neighboring pixels that share similar properties. The similarities could be in terms of the texture, color, or shape. This region-growing approach is based on similarities, whereas the edge-based techniques are totally dependent on the dissimilarities. Region-growing methods are preferred over edge-based techniques when it comes to a noisy image, as edges are difficult to detected.

This approach is dependent on the examination of the neighboring pixels. Then, they are merged to seed, then growth occurs. This is an iterative process and will keep growing until the strong edges are identified, i.e., discontinuity is identified.

Algorithm

1. Start with a set of seed points.
2. A similarity check has to be carried out between the seed region of the considered points and the candidate pixel.
3. If the similarity is as per the set threshold or below, grow regions by appending that pixel to the seed region. Keep iterating until the discontinuity is identified.

An example is presented for better understanding. The input image is presented to undergo the region-growing process. The seed is identified and, in this case, we have identified it as 1:

1	1	5	6	5	5
2	(1)	6	7	4	6
3	2	7	4	6	7
1	0	5	5	7	6
2	0	4	6	8	5
0	1	6	4	5	8

Seeds Identification – 1 is the seed

Next, the threshold has to be set and in this case it is 3:

1	1	5	6	5	5
2	(1)	6	7	4	6
3	2	7	4	6	7
1	0	5	5	7	6
2	0	4	6	8	5
0	1	6	4	5	8

Criteria - Threshold set to 3

The growth occurs after the comparison, i.e., 1 is compared with all its neighbors. The regions are identified as follows:

1	1	5	6	5	5
2	1	6	7	4	6
3	2	7	4	6	7
1	0	5	5	7	6
2	0	4	6	8	5
0	1	6	4	5	8

Region - 1   Region - 2

1	1	5	6	5	5
2	(1)	6	7	4	6
3	2	7	4	6	7
1	0	5	5	7	6
2	0	4	6	8	5
0	1	6	4	5	8

Criteria - Threshold set to 3

The final output is as follows:

Region b			Region b		
a	a	b	b	b	b
a	a	b	b	b	b
a	a	b	b	b	b
a	a	b	b	b	b
a	a	b	b	b	b
a	a	b	b	b	b

Output Image

This is an iterative process and there can be more than one seed.

6.5.2 Region Split-and-Merge Technique

Now it is time to visualize how the region split-and-merge technique works. It is interesting and easier.

Region splitting is the opposite of region growing. The idea of region splitting is to split any region successively into four disjoint quadrants. When no further splitting is possible, merge any adjacent regions. Stop when no further merging is possible. An example is provide next. The approach is referred to as top-down, and in case the bottom-up approach is followed, it is referred to as the region-merging technique.

Let us go through the region-splitting technique step by step:

1. Determine if the similar pixels can be grouped together.
2. If the pixels do not meet the requirement and they cannot be grouped with other pixels, then the region has to be subdivided. The division should be into four equal quadrants.
3. This is an iterative process and it will go on until the conditions are met.
4. In Figure 6.8, the b, c, and d regions are simple and they have similar pixels. So no further processing is required. But region a has dissimilar pixels inside and has to be further divided into four quadrants. This will go on until the conditions are met and no further subdivisions are possible. Now if all the pixels in a particular region satisfy some common property in that region, then splitting is stopped.

Sometimes, a numerical example is easier to understand. Assume the following matrix as the input 8 × 8 image. With the region-splitting method, the image will be processed. The threshold is to be considered, and Zmax – Zmin should be 3, the assumed threshold (i.e., the maximum value, Zmax,

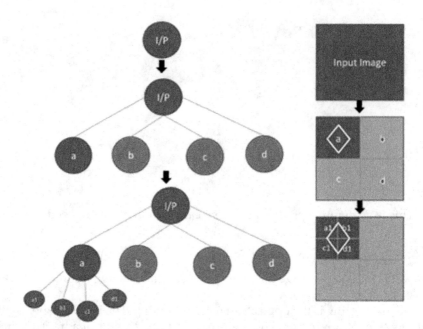

FIGURE 6.8
Region-splitting technique.

of a pixel in a region minus the minimum value of a pixel, Zmin, in the same region should not exceed 3).

$$f(x,y) = \begin{bmatrix} 5 & 6 & 6 & 6 & 4 & 7 & 6 & 6 \\ 6 & 7 & 6 & 7 & 5 & 5 & 4 & 7 \\ 6 & 6 & 4 & 4 & 3 & 2 & 5 & 6 \\ 5 & 4 & 5 & 4 & 2 & 3 & 4 & 6 \\ 0 & 3 & 2 & 3 & 3 & 2 & 4 & 7 \\ 0 & 0 & 0 & 0 & 2 & 2 & 5 & 6 \\ 1 & 1 & 0 & 1 & 0 & 3 & 4 & 4 \\ 1 & 0 & 1 & 0 & 2 & 3 & 5 & 4 \end{bmatrix}$$

After splitting into four quadrants, it will look like

$$f(x,y) = \left[\begin{array}{cccc|cccc} 5 & 6 & 6 & 6 & 4 & 7 & 6 & 6 \\ 6 & 7 & 6 & 7 & 5 & 5 & 4 & 7 \\ 6 & 6 & 4 & 4 & 3 & 2 & 5 & 6 \\ 5 & 4 & 5 & 4 & 2 & 3 & 4 & 6 \\ \hline 0 & 3 & 2 & 3 & 3 & 2 & 4 & 7 \\ 0 & 0 & 0 & 0 & 2 & 2 & 5 & 6 \\ 1 & 1 & 0 & 1 & 0 & 3 & 4 & 4 \\ 1 & 0 & 1 & 0 & 2 & 3 & 5 & 4 \end{array} \right]$$

The first region is processed, identified as R_1.

$$R_1$$

$$\begin{bmatrix} 5 & 6 & 6 & 6 \\ 6 & 7 & 6 & 7 \\ 6 & 6 & 4 & 4 \\ 5 & 4 & 5 & 4 \end{bmatrix}$$

Here,

Zmax = 7

Zmin = 4

T = 3

$$|Zmax - Zmin| <= T \,(\text{Condition to be met})$$

$|7-4| <= 3$, The entire region R1 satisfies the condition and hence does not require further split.

Let us proceed with the second region, R_2:

$$R_2$$

$$\begin{bmatrix} 4 & 7 & 6 & 6 \\ 5 & 5 & 4 & 7 \\ 3 & 2 & 5 & 6 \\ 2 & 3 & 4 & 6 \end{bmatrix}$$

Here,

Zmax = 7

Zmin = 2

$|Zmax - Zmin| <= 3$ is the precondition.

The condition is NOT met and hence further subdivision is inevitable.

$$R_2$$

R_{21}		R_{22}	
4	7	6	6
5	5	4	7
3	2	5	6
2	3	4	6
R_{23}		R_{24}	

As earlier, the rest of the computation is carried out.

6.6 Edge-Based Segmentation

Edge detection is a very important topic for discussion and edge-based segmentation is considered very effective too. It is a process through which the edges are located leading to identification of the objects in the image. If the edges are correctly identified, one can retrieve significant information. Let us first understand something fundamental about edge detection. It is about detecting the edges in the image, which is based on the discontinuity in the color or texture or saturation. Fundamentally, it is discontinuity in the features. To increase the accuracy and to improvise the results, more processing becomes inevitable. Concatenating the edges to form the edge chains is the most followed solution that helps in identifying borders in the image.

See Chapter 4 for more details about edge detection.

6.7 Clustering-Based Segmentation

Clustering helps in dividing the complete data to multiple clusters. Simply, it is a method or technique to group data into clusters. The objects inside a cluster should/must have high similarity. A detailed understanding of the topic can be found in Chapter 7, Section 7.5.

6.8 Morphological Transforms-Based Segmentation

Morphology is a branch in biology that deals with the form and structure of animals and plants. Similarly, mathematical morphology is used as a tool for extracting image components that are useful in the representation and description of region shape. The image components that are useful in shape representation and description are boundaries, skeletons, and convex hulls. The field of mathematical morphology contributes a wide range of operators to image processing and these operators are based on a few simple mathematical concepts from set theory. These operators are called morphological operators and are particularly useful for the analysis of binary images. Common applications of morphological operators include edge detection, noise removal, image enhancement, and image segmentation.

Morphological operators often take a binary image and a structuring element as input and combine them using a set operator (intersection, union, inclusion, complement). These operators process objects in the input image based on characteristics of its shape, and this shape information is encoded in the structuring element. Initially, morphological operators could be applied only on binary images, and the basic operations were dilation and erosion. Natural extension using maximum and minimum operations brings morphologic transformations from binary image processing to grayscale image processing. In some image analysis and machine vision applications, such as industrial defect inspection or biomedical imaging, segmentation based on thresholding or edge detection is not sufficient because the image quality is insufficient or the objects under inspection touch or overlap. In such applications, morphological segmentation is an effective method for image segmentation. Under morphological segmentation, there are many technical items to be discussed. They are referred to as morphological operations and are listed as follows:

- Dilation and erosion
- Opening and closing
- Hit-or-miss transform

Before diving deeper, it is important to understand and to recall some fundamentals of set theory. Table 6.1 summarizes set theory.

Consider two sets A and B. Some of the basic operations with sets are union, intersection, compliment, reflection, translation, and difference. These basic operations are described in Table 6.1 and shown in Figure 6.9. Also, the basic logical operations between two sets are presented diagrammatically in Figure 6.10.

6.8.1 Dilation and Erosion

Dilation is the process through which probing and expanding the shapes inside the image happens. One can connect the dilation process with the local maximum filter. In other words, it adds a layer of pixels on the object boundaries. Morphological dilation makes objects more visible and even it fills in the small holes in the objects. This certainly improves visibility.

TABLE 6.1

Basic Set Operations

Set Operation	Result
Union	$A \cup B$, which contains all the elements in set A and set B.
Intersection	$A \cap B$, which contains the elements that are present in both set A and set B.
Compliment	Ac, which contains complement of elements in set A, i.e., 1s in set A will become 0s in set Ac. Similarly, 0s in set A will become 1s in set Ac.
Reflection	Reflection of set $B \equiv ww = -b \; \forall \; b \in B$
Difference	$A - B = A \cap Bc$
Translation	Translation of set $A = (A)z = ww = a + z \; \forall \; a \in A$

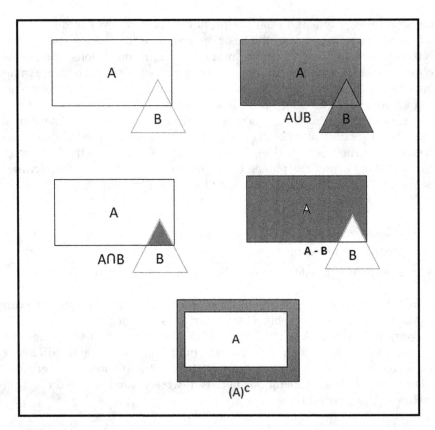

FIGURE 6.9
Basic set operations.

Erosion is the opposite of the dilation process. Erosion removes pixels on object boundaries. It acts like a local minimum filter, removing a layer of pixels from the boundaries. Erosion is effectively seen as a thinning operation. Morphological erosion removes islands and small objects so that only substantive objects remain. Figure 6.11 reveals the impact of erosion and dilation on an input image.

A simpler comparison of dilation with erosion is shown through the following points:

- Dilation is all about increasing the size of the object, as it is the addition of pixels. But erosion is decreasing the size of the object.
- Dilation fills the holes and disconnected areas, whereas erosion removes the smallest of the anomalies.
- Dilation is "a XOR b", whereas erosion is a dual of dilation.

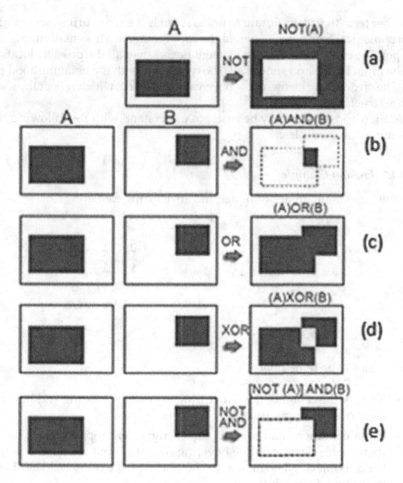

FIGURE 6.10
Basic logical operations between two sets A and B. (a) Compliment of A. (b) Logical AND operation between two sets A and B. (c) Logical OR operation between two sets A and B. (d) EXOR operation between sets A and B. (e) Logical AND operation between compliment of A and B sets.

FIGURE 6.11
From left, the sample input image, the dilated image, and the eroded image.

Another term that is important to understand is the structuring element. The morphological techniques operate the input image with a small matrix (i.e., shape). The chosen structuring element hovers over all the possible locations in the input image and should also be compared with the neighborhood pixels. The structuring element can have values of 0 or 1, which reflect the shape of the structuring element.

Dilation and erosion may be easier to understand with the following simple numerical examples.

6.8.1.1 Erosion Example

Assume the following input image and structuring element:

0	0	0	0	0
0	1	1	1	0
0	1	1	1	0
0	1	1	1	0
0	1	1	1	0

Input Image

0	1	0
1	1	1
0	1	0

Structuring Element

The rules to be remembered are:

- Identify the center of the structuring element by holding and hovering it over the input image.
- If the condition matches, i.e., center, right, left, top, bottom of the structuring element, while hovering over the input image and if all the cells match when fit over the input image, the cell should get 1 as the output. Else, it is 0.

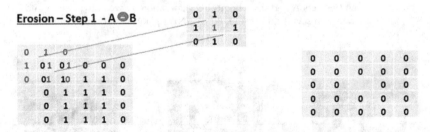

So, it is simple! Let's check the neighbors, as one could see, most of the slots would get 0 other than the center position of the input image.

The first step is presented – the center of the structuring element – i.e., 1 should be kept as the reference mark and should be picked and moved over the input image. The results should be 0 if the 1s do not match. However, here most of the cells get 0s, as it could not meet the condition of 1s in the structuring element getting matched to 1s in the input image. Hence, it is a 0.

Erosion – The 1's case

0	0	0	0	0
0	1	11	1	0
0	11	11	11	0
0	1	11	1	0
0	1	1	1	0

0	1	0
1	1	1
0	1	0

0	0	0	0	0
0	0	0	0	0
0	0	1	0	0
0	0	0	0	0
0	0	0	0	0

One can understand that all the 1s in structuring element get a match when hovered over the input image while the operation is carried out in the prescribed region. Since it is a match, it is 1.

Erosion, essentially, reduces the number of 1s in the input matrix.

So, the final eroded result is

0	0	0	0	0
0	0	0	0	0
0	0	1	0	0
0	0	0	0	0
0	0	0	0	0

It is now time to understand how exactly dilation happens. We shall consider the same set of inputs and structuring elements for the process.

6.8.1.2 Dilation Example: A Dilated with B

0	0	0	0	0
0	1	1	1	0
0	1	1	1	0
0	1	1	1	0
0	1	1	1	0

0	1	0
1	1	1
0	1	1

Structuring Element

Input Image

Identify the center of the structuring element by holding and hovering it over the input image. If the condition matches, i.e., center, right, left, top, bottom of the structuring element, while hovering over the input image and if any one of the cells match the value, then it is a 1. Else, it is a 0. The entire process is presented pictorially in the following.

```
0  0  0  0  0
0  1  1  1  0          0  1  0
0  1  1  1  0          1  1  1
0  1  1  1  0          0  1  1
0  1  1  1  0       Structuring Element
     Input Image
```

The Process, Step by step:

```
0  0  0  0  0          0  1  0          0
0  1  1  1  0          1  1  1
0  1  1  1  0          0  1  1
0  1  1  1  0
0  1  1  1  0
```

```
0  0  0  0  0          0  1  0          0  1
0  1  1  1  0          1  1  1
0  1  1  1  0          0  1  1
0  1  1  1  0
0  1  1  1  0
```

```
0  0  0  0  0          0  1  0          0  1  1
0  1  1  1  0          1  1  1
0  1  1  1  0          0  1  1
0  1  1  1  0
0  1  1  1  0
```

```
0  0  0  0  0          0  1  0          0  1  1  1
0  1  1  1  0          1  1  1
0  1  1  1  0          0  1  1
0  1  1  1  0
0  1  1  1  0
```

```
0  0  0  0  0                           0  1  1  1  0
0  1  1  1  0          0  1  0
0  1  1  1  0          1  1  1
0  1  1  1  0          0  1  1
0  1  1  1  0
```

```
0  0  0  0  0                           0  1  1  1  0
0  1  1  1  0          0  1  0          1
0  1  1  1  0          1  1  1
0  1  1  1  0          0  1  1
0  1  1  1  0
```

```
                    0  1  1  1  0
                    1  1  1  1
                       1  1  1          All the one's will
                       1  1  1          be respected
                       1  1  1
```

```
0  0  0  0  0                           0  1  1  1  0
0  1  1  1  0          0  1  0          1  1  1  1
0  1  1  1  0          1  1  1          1  1  1  1
0  1  1  1  0          0  1  1             1  1  1
0  1  1  1  0                              1  1  1
```

```
0 0 0 0 0                      0 1 1 1 0
0 1 1 1 0        0 1 0         1 1 1 1
0 1 1 1 0        1 1 1         1 1 1 1
0 1 1 1 0        0 1 1         1 1 1 1
0 1 1 1 0                        1 1 1


0 0 0 0 0                      0 1 1 1 0
0 1 1 1 0        0 1 0         1 1 1 1
0 1 1 1 0        1 1 1         1 1 1 1
0 1 1 1 0        0 1 1         1 1 1 1
0 1 1 1 0                      1 1 1 1


0 0 0 0 0                      0 1 1 1 0
0 1 1 1 0        0 1 0         1 1 1 1
0 1 1 1 0        1 1 1         1 1 1 1
0 1 1 1 0        0 1 1         1 1 1 1
0 1 1 1 0                      1 1 1 1


0 0 0 0 0                      0 1 1 1 0
0 1 1 1 0        0 1 0         1 1 1 1 1
0 1 1 1 0        1 1 1         1 1 1 1
0 1 1 1 0        0 1 1         1 1 1 1
0 1 1 1 0                        1 1 1


0 0 0 0 0                      0 1 1 1 0
0 1 1 1 0        0 1 0         1 1 1 1 1
0 1 1 1 0        1 1 1         1 1 1 1 1
0 1 1 1 0        0 1 1         1 1 1 1
0 1 1 1 0                      1 1 1


0 0 0 0 0                      0 1 1 1 0
0 1 1 1 0        0 1 0         1 1 1 1 1
0 1 1 1 0        1 1 1         1 1 1 1 1
0 1 1 1 0        0 1 1         1 1 1 1 1
0 1 1 1 0                      1 1 1 1


0 0 0 0 0                      0 1 1 1 0
0 1 1 1 0        0 1 0         1 1 1 1 1
0 1 1 1 0        1 1 1         1 1 1 1 1
0 1 1 1 0        0 1 1         1 1 1 1 1
0 1 1 1 0                      1 1 1 1 1
```

The number of 1s is increased when the dilation process is performed.

6.8.2 Opening and Closing

These two are very important operations to be noted. Let us start with opening, followed by closing.

Opening is erosion followed by dilation. It is denoted by ∘. The process of eroding an image followed by dilating is done in order to remove any narrow connections or lines between two regions in an image. The erosion and the dilation have to be carried out with the same structuring element. By carrying out the morphological opening operation, one can remove the smaller objects from an image while retaining the larger objects. It is represented with the expression $A \circ B = (A \ominus B) \oplus B$. Refer to Figure 6.12 for a pictorial representation.

Closing is dilation followed by erosion. The process of dilation and erosion should be carried out with the same structuring element. This process is very handy for filling the small holes, while also preserving the shape and size of the objects present in the image. Refer to Figure 6.13 to visualize the impact of the closing operation. Closing is represented with the expression: $A \bullet B = (A \oplus B) \ominus B$.

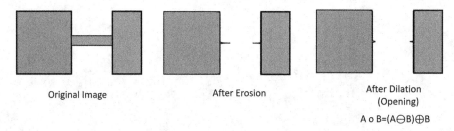

Original Image   After Erosion   After Dilation
                                                                 (Opening)

                                                          $A \circ B = (A \ominus B) \oplus B$

FIGURE 6.12
Opening operation.

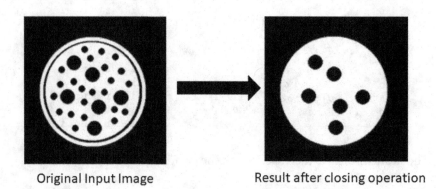

Original Input Image   Result after closing operation

FIGURE 6.13
Closing operation.

6.8.3 Hit-or-Miss Transform

A simple approach, the hit-or-miss transform can be deployed when a particular pattern in the foreground and background is searched for. If there is a match, it is a hit. If not, it is a miss. The following examples further explain the concept.

Let us assume the structuring and input image (in the form of a matrix) as shown next:

0	0	0
X	1	X
1	1	1

Structuring element

The structuring element has 1s and 0s, and there are some X cells as well. They are referred to as "don't cares" and they don't have be considered. The input to be worked out with the structuring element is presented next as case 1.

0	0	0
1	1	0
1	1	1

Input Case 1

For the hit scenario, all the considered 1s in the structuring element should match with the 1s in the input image. All the considered 0s should also match with the 0s in the input image. Don't cares can be ignored. So, having said that, all the 1s in the following structuring element and input go hand in hand, and hence this is a hit; people also call it "true":

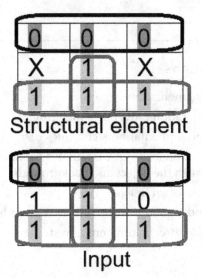

Structural element

Input

In the next scenario has different input for the structuring element:

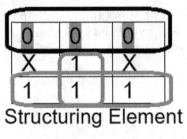

Structuring Element

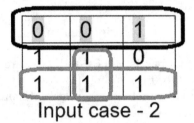

Input case - 2

Here, as one can see, it is a miss. The 1s highlighted in the input and structuring element match. However, the highlighted 0s in the structuring element do not match with the input elements, and hence is declared a miss. This is also termed "false".

The concepts of segmentation have been dealt with in this chapter. Now, we can move ahead to the next chapter to learn the difference between regression and classification, discuss a few classification algorithms, and explore clustering.

6.9 Review Questions

1. Define image segmentation.
2. Why can segmentation often be challenging?
3. List the types of segmentation techniques discussed in this chapter.
4. Which segmentation technique is suitable for images with a distinct difference between the object and background?
5. Define histogram of an image.
6. How do you find a good threshold from a given histogram?
7. When is multiple thresholding employed?
8. Define edges.

9. Differentiate dilation and erosion.

10. When do you use the morphological operation hit-or-miss transform?

11. What is region-based segmentation?

12. Compare the region-growing approach to edge-based techniques.

6.9.1 Answers

1. Image segmentation is a process through which one could partition a given image into multiple subgroups based on common properties, such as intensity or texture.

2. Segmentation is challenging because of the variability in the shapes of the objects of interest and variability in the quality of the input image. The quality may be poor due to multiple factors, such as non-uniform lighting, shadows, noise, overlap among objects, and poor contrast between objects and background.

3. The types of segmentation techniques are thresholding technique segmentation, histogram-based segmentation, region-based segmentation, edge-based segmentation, clustering-based segmentation, morphological transforms, and texture-based segmentation approaches.

4. Thresholding method.

5. The histogram of an image is a plot between intensity levels (i.e., gray levels) along the x-axis and number (frequency) of pixels at each gray level along the y-axis.

6. A good threshold can be found from the histogram if the histogram peak is tall, narrow, symmetric, and separated by deep valleys. A good threshold is the intensity value that is chosen from the bottom of the valley of the histogram.

7. Multiple thresholding is employed when there are two light objects on a dark background in an image.

8. Edges are defined as "sudden and significant changes in the intensity" of an image. These changes happen between the boundaries of an object in an image.

9. Dilation is the process through which the probing and expanding of shapes inside the image happens, i.e., it adds a layer of pixels on the object boundaries. Erosion removes pixels on object boundaries, i.e., a layer of pixels from the boundaries can be removed to decrease the size of the object. This is opposite to the dilation process.

10. The hit-or-miss transform can be used when a particular pattern in the foreground and background are searched for. If there is a match, it is a hit. If not, that it is a miss.

11. The region-based segmentation method segments the image into various regions having similar characteristics. A region is a group of connected pixels with similar properties.

12. The region-growing approach is based on similarities, whereas edge-based techniques are dependent on dissimilarities. Region-growing methods are preferred over edge-based techniques when it comes to noisy images, as edges would be difficult to detect.

Further Reading

Ashburner, J. and Friston, K.J., 2005. Unified segmentation. *Neuroimage, 26*(3), pp. 839–851.

Haralick, R.M. and Shapiro, L.G., 1985. Image segmentation techniques. *Computer Vision, Graphics, and Image Processing, 29*(1), pp. 100–132.

Pal, N.R. and Pal, S.K., 1993. A review on image segmentation techniques. *Pattern Recognition, 26*(9), pp. 1277–1294.

Tautz, D., 2004. Segmentation. *Developmental Cell, 7*(3), pp. 301–312.

Wind, Y., 1978. Issues and advances in segmentation research. *Journal of Marketing Research, 15*(3), pp. 317–337.

Yanowitz, S.D. and Bruckstein, A.M., 1989. A new method for image segmentation. *Computer Vision, Graphics, and Image Processing, 46*(1), pp. 82–95.

7

Classification: A Must-Know Concept

Learning Objectives

After reading this chapter, the reader should have a clear understanding about:

- (SVMs)
- Terms used in SVMs
- How SVMs work?
- k-Nearest neighbors (k-NN)
- Clustering
- k-Means clustering

7.1 Introduction

The first question normally arises this way: What is the difference between regression and classification? Regression and classification both fall under the heading of supervised learning algorithms. Both have extensive usage in machine learning (ML) and both use a labeled data set. Then, where are they different? The problems that they solve are different.

Regression predicts continuous values, for example, salaries, grades, and ages. Classification classifies things, such as into male/female, pass/fail, false/true, spam/legitimate. Classification divides the given data set into classes based on the parameters considered. An example will be very helpful.

Let's take Gmail. Gmail classifies email as legit or spam. The model is trained with millions of emails and has many parameters to consider. Whenever a new email pops up, the classifications considered include inbox, spam, promotions, and updates. If the email is spam, it goes to spam folder. If it is legit, it goes to the inbox.

There are many famous and frequently used classification algorithms. They include:

- Support vector machine (SVM)
- k-Nearest neighbor (k-NN)
- Kernel SVM
- Logistic regression
- Naïve Bayes
- Decision tree classification
- Random forest classification

It is good to understand and learn all of them, but that would be out of the scope for this book. So, we handpicked support vector machine and k-nearest neighbor for discussion.

7.2 Support Vector Machine (SVM)

To start with, the SVM is very easy to use and to learn. Data scientists claim that the SVM offers better accuracy than other classifiers. SVMs are often used in email classification and handwriting recognition.

An SVM is usable for both regression and classification problems. But, most commonly it is used for classification problems over regression. The main aim or target of the SVM is creating an optimum line or a decision boundary. The decision boundary allows segregating the data set into classes. Also, new data upon entry can be correctly classified as well in the future.

The appropriate decision boundary is referred to as the hyperplane. It is very important to understand the terms used with SVMs and some of them are presented in the next sections.

7.2.1 Hyperplane

A hyperplane is a plane that separates (i.e., enables grouping) objects that belong to different classes. This line helps in classifying the data points, e.g., the stars and triangles in Figure 7.1.

The dimension of a hyperplane is a variable too. Figure 7.1 has two features and hence one straight line is sufficient. If there are three features, there has to be a two-dimensional plane.

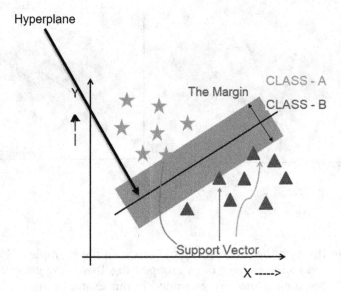

FIGURE 7.1
SVM – The complete picture.

7.2.2 Support Vectors

Refer again to Figure 7.1. The red stars and green triangles are the support vectors. These points are very close to the hyperplane. As vectors, these data points affect the position and placement of the hyperplane.

7.2.3 Margin

The margin is a gap. If the margin between two classes is large, then it is a good margin; otherwise it is considered bad. In simple terms, the margin is the gap between the closest points of two lines. Using Figure 7.1, one can understand that the margin can be calculated as the perpendicular distance from the line to the support vectors (red stars and green triangles).

7.3 How SVMs Work?

First, group/segregate the data set (i.e., nonclassified to classified) in the best possible way. The next task is simple. Select/draw a hyperplane with the maximum margin between the support vectors from the input data set. The more the margin, the larger the gap.

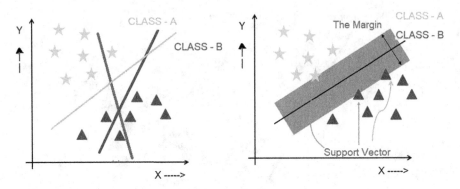

FIGURE 7.2
Hyperplane selection.

Let's go through the process step by step with the example of Figure 7.2. The stars and triangles have been grouped together. Now generate hyperplanes. Three such planes are generated in our example: brown, blue, and red. The brown and blue have failed miserably to classify. This reflects a high error rate. However, red is very apt and it does the separation properly. So, what do we do? Choose the best line. The best drawn line is presented as a black line on the right side of the Figure 7.2.

That is, it. One can now understand that all the red stars and green triangles are grouped appropriately based on the hyperplane.

The complete implementation and a quick lecture on the SVM can be found at https://youtu.be/Qd9Aj_EMfk0.

7.4 k-Nearest Neighbor (k-NN)

The k-NN algorithm is one of the easiest and most frequently used approaches like SVM. k-NN is also based on supervised learning. Based on history, the current case is predicted, i.e., when new data is sent in for classification, based on the similarity of data available in the past, the new data is classified into the most similar category. In simple words, new data can be classified with ease into the most similar category with k-NN in place.

The next question is where to use k-NN. It has been used for classification and regression. But, like SVM, k-NN also has better results when used with classification.

k-NN has two very important aspects:

- It is referred to as nonparametric.
- It is also said to be a lazy learner algorithm.

It is important to understand what is nonparametric. It means the algorithm does not make any assumptions on the underlying data.

Lazy learning means nothing happens immediately in this approach. The algorithm does not learn anything from the training set at that instance. But it stores the entire data set during the classification and then does the action on the data set. There is no specialized training phase and the algorithm uses all the data for training while classifying.

For example, if someone wants to classify a fruit or orange, when the input is sent in, the algorithm works with the similarity concept. Based on the similarity of the features, it will now classify the item.

In the k-NN, remember k is king. Data scientists have preferred k to be an odd number when the classes are even. For example, k could be 1, 3, 5, 7, etc. for two classes. Note that when k = 1, it is the nearest neighbor algorithm.

It is now the time to approach the k-NN step by step.

1. Select the k number of neighbors.
2. Calculate the Euclidean distance of the k number of neighbors.
3. Take the k-nearest neighbors as per the calculated Euclidean distance.
4. Start counting. Among these k neighbors, count the number of data points in each category.
5. Assign the new data points to that category for which the number of neighbors is maximum.
6. The model is now ready.

See Figure 7.3 for the start of an example. The problem statement is presented pictorially in Figure 7.4. The new data entry has to be classified as a red star or a green triangle.

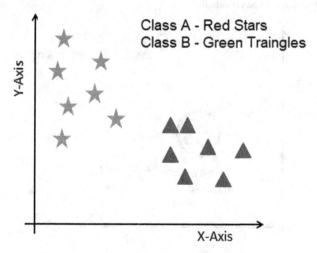

FIGURE 7.3
Assumed scenario.

Case 1: If k is chosen as 1, then the task becomes easier and it is the simplest option. The input data gets classified as Class A. See Figure 7.5.

Case 2: Let us choose k = 3. First, calculate the Euclidean distance between the data points. The Euclidean distance is the distance between two points. (This can be done through other methods too. Python has built-in functions to help programmers.) See Figure 7.6 to understand how k-NN works with the k value chosen as 3.

Case 3: Figure 7.7 shows the scenario when k is set as 7.

By now, readers should understand the way k-NN works. But take note that keeping low k values should be avoided as the prediction could go wrong.

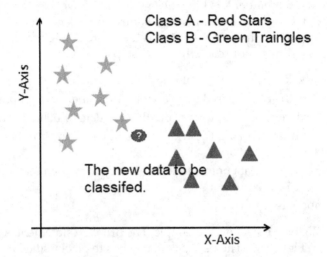

FIGURE 7.4
The assumed scenario to be classified.

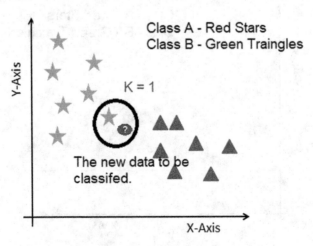

FIGURE 7.5
Case 1: k = 1.

- Class A = 1 count
- Class B = 2 count.
- So, naturally, the new entry is classified as B. (I.e. green triangles)

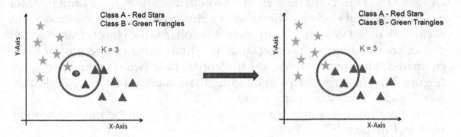

FIGURE 7.6
Case 2: k = 3.

- Class A = 4 count
- Class B = 3 count.
- So, naturally, the new entry is classified as A. (I.e. Red Stars)

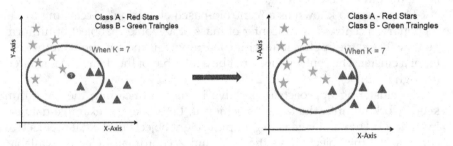

FIGURE 7.7
Case 3: k = 7.

Advantages of k-NN include:

- It is simple.
- The more data, the better the classification.

Disadvantages include:

- Finding the optimum value for k is challenging.

You can find a brief lecture about k-NN from the authors at https://youtu.be/nVgZbVUmh50.

The next topic for discussion is clustering, a very important and interesting area to learn about.

7.5 Clustering: An Interesting Concept to Know

To make it simple, clustering is a method or technique to group data into clusters. The objects inside a cluster should/must have high similarity, for example, medical students – first year is a cluster, second year is a cluster, etc. A cluster's objects should be definitely dissimilar to the objects from another cluster, for example, engineering students – first year is another cluster when compared with first-year medical students). These two clusters are disjoint (Figure 7.8). Clustering helps in dividing the complete data to multiple clusters. This is a non-labeled approach.

It is time to understand k-means clustering, one of the most commonly used techniques.

7.5.1 k-Means Clustering

In clustering, the metric being employed is similarity! It is the metric that measures the relationship between the objects. Why do we need clustering? Simple, it gives you an exploratory view of the data. One could get better idea about the data with clustering.

k-Means is also known as a "centroid-based clustering". According to the dictionary, a centroid is the center of mass of a geometric object of uniform density. The same applies to machine learning; it is the data point at the center of a cluster. The centroid need not be a member of the data set considered (though it can be).

This clustering approach is iterative in nature, meaning the algorithm keeps working until the target is achieved. Let's take the example data set in Table 7.1. The challenge is to group the eight objects in the data set as two clusters. All the objects have the X, Y, and Z coordinates clearly available. How do we select the k value? K is the number of clusters. Here, it is 2. So, let us set the k value as 2.

Initially, we have to take any two centroids. Why go with two centroids? Since the k value is 2, the number of centroids chosen is also 2. Once chosen,

Cluster – A (Medical Students – I Year)   Cluster – B (Engineering Students – I Year)

FIGURE 7.8
An example of clustering.

TABLE 7.1

Data Set Considered for Clustering

Object	X	Y	Z
O1	1	4	1
O2	1	2	2
O3	1	4	2
O4	2	1	2
O5	1	1	1
O6	2	4	2
O7	1	1	2
O8	2	1	1

the data points are tagged to any of the clusters based on the distance. It is time to start the computation.

- First centroid = O2. This will be cluster 1. (O2 = First centroid = 1, 2, 2).
- Second centroid = O6. This will be cluster 2. (O6 = Second centroid = 2, 4, 2).

Can we choose any other object as the centroid? This is a very common question and, yes, any object can become a centroid.

How do we measure distance? There is a formula to the rescue:

$$D = |x2 - x1| + |y2 - y1| + |z2 - z1|$$

where D is the distance between two objects. People call it the Manhattan distance.

Remember, any object has X, Y, Z coordinates as per the data set! So, the task is simple. It is time to reconstruct the table and one has to use the distance between each object and the centroids chosen.

Like O1, O2, and O3, the rest of the calculations to find the distance from C1 and C2 are to be computed. Refer to Table 7.2 for a clearer understanding.

The next step is to go ahead with the clustering. This is based on the distance, whichever is shorter. Say C1 is shorter than C2 for an object, then the object falls to C1. Hence, the clustering should look like Table 7.3.

For a clear understanding, the following color guidelines were followed in Table 7.3. Cluster 1 is represented by green color and cluster 2 is represented by red. Also refer to Table 7.4.

In the next round, the next iteration has to be done. Hence, the new clusters will be as in Table 7.5.

So, we can stop here. No updates in the centroids or changes in the cluster grouping have been observed. Hence, this is the correct clustering. This is how k-means clustering works. For more information, watch the lecture

TABLE 7.2

Distance from C1 and C2

Object	X	Y	Z	Distance from C1 (1, 2, 2)	Distance from C2 (2, 4, 2)
O1	1	4	1	$D = |1–1| + |4–2| + |2–1| = 3$	$D = |1–1| + |4–2| + |2–1| = 2$
O2	1	2	2	$D = |1–1| + |2–2| + |2–2| = 0$	$D = |2–1| + |4–2| + |2–2| = 3$
O3	1	4	2	$D = |1–1| + |4–2| + |2–2| = 2$	$D = |2–1| + |4–4| + |2–2| = 1$
O4	2	1	2	2	3
O5	1	1	1	2	5
O6	2	4	2	3	0
O7	1	1	2	1	4
O8	2	1	1	3	4

TABLE 7.3

Clustering

Cluster 1
OB-2 (0 < 3)
OB-4 (2 < 3)
OB-5 (2 < 5)
OB-7 (1 < 4)
OB-8 (3 < 4)

Cluster 2
OB-1 (3 >2)
OB-3 (2 >1)
OB-6 (3 >0)

Objects	X	Y	Z	Distance from C1(1,2,2)	Distance from C2(2,4,2)
O1	1	4	1	$D= |1-1|+|4-2|+|2-1|= 3$	$D= |1-1|+|4-2|+|2-1|=2$
O2	1	2	2	$D= |1-1|+|2-2|+|2-2|=0$	$D= |2-1|+|4-2|+|2-2|= 3$
O3	1	4	2	$D= |1-1|+|4-2|+|2-2|=2$	$D= |2-1|+|4-4|+|2-2|=1$
O4	2	1	2	2	3
O5	1	1	1	2	5
O6	2	4	2	3	0
O7	1	1	2	1	4
O8	2	1	1	3	4

TABLE. 7.4

Clusters 1 and 2

Objects	X	Y	Z
01	1	4	1
02	1	2	2
03	1	4	2
04	2	1	2
05	1	1	1
06	2	4	2
07	1	1	2
08	2	1	1

- **Cluster 1:** ((1+2+1+1+2)/5, (2+1+1+1+1)/5, (2+2+1+2+1)/5) = (1.4, 1.2, 1.6)
- **Cluster 2:** ((1+1+2)/3, (4+4+4)/3, (1+2+2)/3) = (1.33, 4, 1.66)

TABLE 7.5

Reiterated Results

Objects	X	Y	Z	Distance from C1(1.4,1.2,1.6)	Distance from C2(1.33, 4, 1.66)
O1	1	4	1	3.8 (1.4 -1 + 4 – 1.2 + 1.6 -1)	1 (1.33 – 1 + 4 – 4 + 1.66 – 1)
O2	1	2	2	1.6 (1.4- 1+ 2 – 1.2 + 2 – 1.6)	2.66 (1.33 – 1+ 4 – 2 + 2 – 1.66)
O3	1	4	2	3.6	0.66
O4	2	1	2	1.2	4
O5	1	1	1	1.2	4
O6	2	4	2	3.8	1
O7	1	1	2	1	3.66
O8	2	1	1	1.4	4.33

by the authors on k-means clustering at https://youtu.be/Fuq9Dw43co0. For more on the way a model has to be developed, see https://youtu.be/6d6HcLG6lFQ.

We have come to the end of this chapter about the fundamentals of machine learning and classification. The video links should be helpful as well. Following are some key points to remember.

TABLE 7.6

New Clusters

Cluster 1
O2
O4
O5
O7
O8

Cluster 2
O1
O3
O6

Key points to remember

- If machines can exhibit intelligence and act like we do, it is called artificial intelligence.
- Machine learning (ML) enables systems to perform a specific task without explicit interventions or inputs.
- In deep learning, the human brain is imitated in processing and understanding the data. Solutions are also processed in a way the brain thinks.
- There are four categories of ML algorithms (some say three, but we make it four for enhanced understanding and clarity):
  - Supervised learning – The data should enable examples and specify outcomes for each situation. Training data is used to build the model, which will predict the outcome for the new data.
  - Unsupervised learning – This approach does not have the knowledge of the outcome variable in the data set.
  - Reinforced learning – The reinforcement algorithm is about feedback-based learning.
  - Evolutionary learning – Evolutionary learning algorithms imitate natural evolution to solve a particular problem.
- Machine learning and deep learning require the users to install some tools and libraries.
- Seaborn is a Python data visualization library based on Matplotlib.
- Regression tries to establish a clear relationship between input and output.
- Ordinary least squares is a type of linear least squares method for estimating the unknown parameters in a linear regression model.

- Classification classifies, something like male/female, pass/fail, false/true, spam/legitimate.
- The main aim or target of the SVM is creating an optimum line or a decision boundary.
- A hyperplane is a plane that separates (i.e., enables grouping) objects that belong to different classes.
- k-NN is one of the easiest and most frequently used methods, like SVM.
- Clustering is a method or technique to group data into clusters. The objects inside a cluster should/must have high similarity.

7.6 Quiz

1. Define machine learning.
2. Define deep learning.
3. Where will someone employ machine learning or deep learning?
4. How is regression useful?
5. What is linear regression?
6. How is linear regression different from logistic regression?
7. Differentiate clustering and classification.
8. Clearly explain how a SVM works.
9. Explain the way k-means clustering functions.

Further Reading

Burkov, A., 2019. *The hundred-page machine learning book* (Vol. 1). Canada: Andriy Burkov.

Goldberg, D.E. and Holland, J.H., 1988. *Genetic algorithms and machine learning.*

Goodfellow, I., Bengio, Y. and Courville, A., 2016. Machine learning basics. *Deep Learning*, 1, pp. 98–164.

Jordan, M.I. and Mitchell, T.M., 2015. Machine learning: Trends, perspectives, and prospects. *Science*, 349(6245), pp. 255–260.

Mohri, M., Rostamizadeh, A. and Talwalkar, A., 2018. *Foundations of machine learning*. MIT Press.

Sammut, C. and Webb, G.I., eds., 2011. *Encyclopedia of machine learning*. Springer Science & Business Media.

Shalev-Shwartz, S. and Ben-David, S., 2014. *Understanding machine learning: From theory to algorithms*. Cambridge University Press.

Williams, D. and Hill, J., 2005. *U.S. Patent Application No. 10/939,288*.

Zhang, X.-D., 2020. Machine learning. In *A matrix algebra approach to artificial intelligence* (pp. 223–440). Singapore: Springer.

8

Playing with OpenCV and Python

8.1 Introduction

You have been exposed to image processing concepts in an extensive manner throughout this book and we hope it has been an enjoyable learning experience. For the cherry on top, this chapter shows how to play around with OpenCV and Python. An interesting set of simple programs to help enhance understanding is presented. Also, YouTube links to video lectures by the authors are provided. We request readers try out these programs practically on their respective machines get a feel for the implementation and to wholly learn the concepts.

8.2 Ubuntu and OpenCV Installation

The codes in this chapter are written in Python and run in Ubuntu as the base. Any recent version of Ubuntu should be handy and one can install Ubuntu alongside the Windows operating system by following the video made available by authors via YouTube: www.youtube.com/watch?v=ESO -OttUHk4.

The readers are requested to install Ubuntu as presented next step-by-step. The first step is to install the OpenCV in the Ubuntu. Open the terminal as is shown in the screenshot in Figure 8.1. Here is where we are going to issue series of commands to install OpenCV.

The next immediate step, which is preferred before every installation, is to go with the "sudo apt update". This command reveals the terminal screen shown in Figure 8.2. It may take a few minutes of time for the update, but it is best to carry it out.

The next step is the most important in the entire sequence: installing OpenCV. Issue the command "sudo apt install python3-opencv". It will

FIGURE 8.1
The Ubuntu terminal.

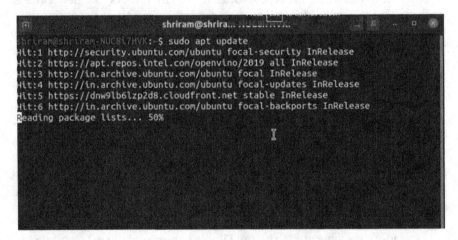

FIGURE 8.2
The sudo apt update step.

complete the installation of the OpenCV and will be done in a couple of minutes. Figure 8.3 is the screenshot presented.

Are we done with the installation? Yes, but it is always best to verify if things have been accomplished correctly. This validation is the next step. The easiest way is to check the version of OpenCV with the command highlighted in Figure 8.4. It will reveal the version of OpenCV installed and only if the installation is correct would you get this result.

FIGURE 8.3
OpenCV installation.

Remember, OpenCV is not a programming language, it is a package. We are going to use Python with OpenCV, and hence we have to import OpenCV in all the programs that are to be demonstrated shortly in the chapter. Readers can also follow the video at the following link to help install OpenCV: https://youtu.be/2DarmQoB9_U to install OpenCV.

It is time to try out some of the simple and interesting image processing exercises with OpenCV and Python. We strongly encourage readers to try this out practically. All the exercises have been supported with demo videos to make the learning easier and complete.

8.3 Image Resizing

Image resizing is all about playing with the pixel counts. It helps in getting a clear result and reducing the computational time.

Let's see a simple code snippet along with results. The function "cv2.resi ze(image, (200, 250))" is where the height and width are specified as part of the function. "Image" is the name of the image file. The complete code is presented in Figure 8.5. The image size is doubled and halved as well. The results are presented in Figure 8.6.

One can also have a look at the video at https://youtu.be/unp5tHxS3Ak to understand the program better.

```
shriram@shriram-NUC8i7HVK:~$ sudo apt install python3-opencv
Reading package lists... Done
Building dependency tree
Reading state information... Done
python3-opencv is already the newest version (4.2.0+dfsg-5).
0 upgraded, 0 newly installed, 0 to remove and 136 not upgraded.
shriram@shriram-NUC8i7HVK:~$ python3 -c "import cv2; print(cv2.__version__)"
4.2.0
shriram@shriram-NUC8i7HVK:~$
shriram@shriram-NUC8i7HVK:~$
```

FIGURE 8.4
The OpenCV installation validation.

```
#!/usr/bin/env python3
import cv2
import numpy as np

image = cv2.imread("flower.jpg", 1)
# Loading the image from the source

bigger = cv2.resize(image, (1000, 1500)
half = cv2.resize(image, (200, 250))
# Here, we pass the Width and height.

cv2.imshow('Original_Image', image)
cv2.imshow('Half_Size', half)
cv2.imshow('Double_Size', bigger)

cv2.waitKey(0)
```

FIGURE 8.5
Image resizing.

8.4 Image Blurring

Blurring helps make the image less clear and the task can be accomplished with filters. Choosing the filters is key for success. But why do we want to blur an image? Simple. It will help in removing the noise. Three types of blurring are generally followed, and all these filters are helpful in removing the noise. The three filters are:

1. Gaussian filter – Removes the Gaussian noise.
2. Median filter – Removes the salt-and-pepper noise.
3. Bilateral filter – Removes noise while retaining edges but is a bit slower.

FIGURE 8.6
Image resizing results.

```
#!/usr/bin/env python3
import cv2
import numpy as np
image = cv2.imread('index.png')

# First, Lets apply the Gaussian filter size 7*7.
Gaussian = cv2.GaussianBlur(image, (7, 7), 0)

# Median Blur, adding 50% noise to original image
median = cv2.medianBlur(image, 5)

# Bilateral filter,
bilat = cv2.bilateralFilter(image,9,75,75)

cv2.imshow('The_Input_Image', image)
cv2.imshow('GaussianBlurredResult', Gaussian)
cv2.imshow('MedianBlurred', median)
cv2.imshow('Bilateral', bilat)
cv2.waitKey(0)
```

FIGURE 8.7
Image blurring with OpenCV.

The three types of blurring can all be implemented with the code in Figure 8.7 and the subsequent results are presented in Figure 8.8. Also one can refer to the video at https://youtu.be/ljfOBTAtRyc for a clearer understanding.

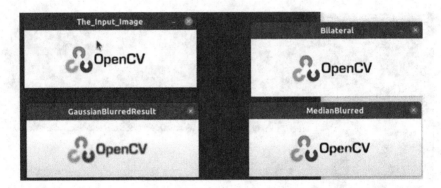

FIGURE 8.8
Image blurring results.

8.5 Image Borders

Drawing borders around an image is simple and interesting. With the method "cv2.copyMakeBorder" one can easily do this. We need to specify the arguments that correspond the number of pixels from the edge to constitute the borders. The code clearly specifies all these and one can have a look at the video at https://youtu.be/JGYdI5uVHi4 to understand things easier. The code is presented in Figure 8.9 followed by the results in Figure 8.10.

```python
#!/usr/bin/env python3
import cv2
import numpy as np

# Reading an image for which we shall add borders.
image = cv2.imread('flower.jpg')

# Can we name it?
window_name = 'The PhotoFramed'

# Using cv2.copyMakeBorder() method
image = cv2.copyMakeBorder(image, 70, 70, 55, 55,cv2.BORDER_REFLECT)

# With the borders!
cv2.imshow(window_name, image)

cv2.waitKey(0)
```

FIGURE 8.9
Image bordering with OpenCV.

FIGURE 8.10
Image bordering.

8.6 Image Conversion to Grayscale Format with OpenCV

Image conversion to grayscale is an easy and interesting exercise one could do. One can easily convert images from the color spaces like RGB (red, green, blue) or HSL (hue, saturation, lightness) to grayscale with OpenCV functions. The code can be written with Python and OpenCV. See Figure 8.11. The results are in Figure 8.12. Also the video lecture at the link https://youtu.be/iIlg5eT35wA should be helpful for a better understanding.

The next exercise is interesting and easy as well. It is edge detection.

8.7 Edge Detection with OpenCV

We have discussed in detail about edges in the previous chapters. It would be excellent if edges could be detected with OpenCV. The piece of code in Figure 8.13 is fully capable of detecting the edges of the given image and we

```
#!/usr/bin/env python3
import cv2
import numpy as np

# Can we load our image? As usual, flower comes to rescue!
image = cv2.imread('flower.jpg')
cv2.imshow('The_Original', image)
cv2.waitKey()

# We shall use cvtColor for the conversion process grayscale
gray_image = cv2.cvtColor(image, cv2.COLOR_BGR2GRAY)

cv2.imshow('Grayscale_Output', gray_image)
cv2.waitKey(0)
```

FIGURE 8.11
Image conversion with OpenCV.

FIGURE 8.12
The input image and grayscale image.

have chosen the Canny edge detector. Results are presented in Figure 8.14. One can view https://youtu.be/YRmiVumcy4I to understand the process in detail.

All the aforementioned exercises are easy enough for anyone to try, and we strongly recommend all readers try them. Similar exercises are available by referring to the playlist created by the authors at https://youtube.com/playlist?list=PL3uLubnzL2Tn3RVU5CywZC17aRGExyZzo.

```
#!/usr/bin/env python3
import cv2
import numpy as np

# Can we load our image? As usual, flower comes to rescue!
image = cv2.imread('flower.jpg')
cv2.imshow('The_Original', image)
cv2.waitKey()

# Canny edge detection.
result = cv2.Canny(image, 100, 200)
cv2.imshow('Edge_Image', result)
cv2.waitKey(0)
```

FIGURE 8.13
Edge detection with the Canny edge detector.

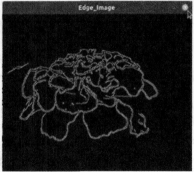

FIGURE 8.14
Input image and detected edges.

8.8 Counting Objects with OpenCV

This section covers a simple way to count objects. In an example, we will count the number of cars moving along a road. The code snippet is provided in Figure 8.15 and the input image is as seen in Figure 8.16. Also the output image with objects detected is as shown in Figure 8.17. The code is fully capable of detecting the objects in the given image.

8.9 Predicting Forest Fire with OpenCV

In this section we will see how we can predict a forest fire from a given data set for both Fire and No Fire classes. The path of the data set is displayed

```
# There are many options for counting objects. here a simple option is chosen
# cvlib library from Python.
!pip install cvlib
import pandas as pd
import numpy as np
import matplotlib.pyplot as plt
import cv2
import cvlib as cv
from cvlib.object_detection import draw_bbox
from numpy.lib.polynomial import poly

%matplotlib inline
```

```
# Can we do some
img = cv2.imread("D:\PPTYT\MachineLearning\CountCars\data\Car_1.JPG")
img = cv2.cvtColor(img, cv2.COLOR_BGR2RGB)
plt.figure(figsize=(15,12))
plt.rc("font", size=12)
plt.title("Input Image", fontsize=24)
plt.imshow(img)
```

```
<matplotlib.image.AxesImage at 0x239410cceb0>
```

```
image = cv2.imread("D:\PPTYT\MachineLearning\CountCars\data\Car_1.JPG")
image = cv2.cvtColor(image, cv2.COLOR_BGR2RGB)
plt.figure(figsize=(20, 20))
box, label, count = cv.detect_common_objects(image)
output = draw_bbox(image, box, label, count)
plt.imshow(output)
plt.show()
print("Number of cars in this image are " +str(label.count('car')))
```

FIGURE 8.15
Counting objects.

in Figures 8.18 and 8.19. The training and validation data set for both Fire and No Fire are also shown in Figure 8.18. The complete code as well as the results are presented in Figure 8.20.

Readers, we have come to the end of the book. This chapter was about simple programs that can aid you in enhancing your level of understanding about image processing. It is hoped the video lectures on YouTube will do the same. We sincerely hope you had an enjoyable as well as an enthralling learning experience.

FIGURE 8.16
Counting objects.

Number of cars in this image are 17

FIGURE 8.17
Counting objects.

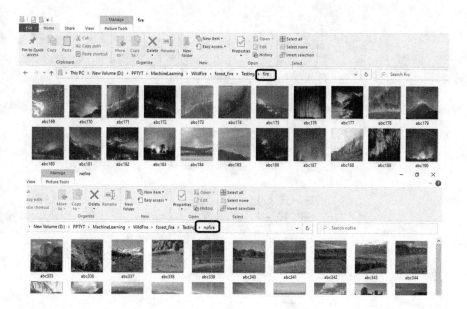

FIGURE 8.18
Data set for Fire and No Fire.

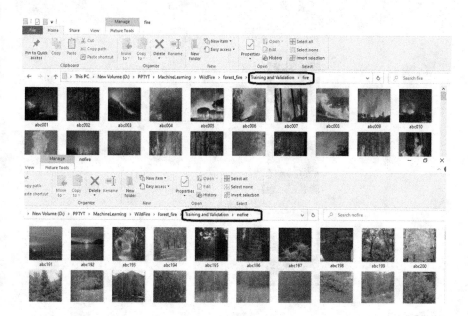

FIGURE 8.19
Training and validation data set for Fire and No Fire.

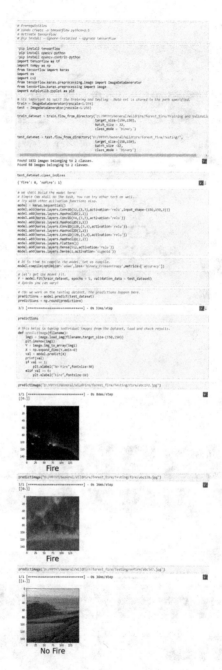

FIGURE 8.20
Code and results for forest fire detection.

Readers have come to the end of this book. This chapter is all about simple programs which can indeed aid the readers to enhance their level of understanding. Also, the same has been presented as video lectures through YouTube by the authors. We sincerely hope to have ensured an enjoyable learning experience.

Index

A

Additive Color Model, 34
Anaconda, 12–15
Analog to digital conversion, 28
Applications of Image Processing, 8

B

Bayer filters, 28
Binary Image, 4, 21, 151
Bits per Pixel, 29
Black-and-white image, 4, 21
Butterworth High-Pass Filter, 121
Butterworth Low-Pass Filter, 113

C

Canny operator, 91
Charge-coupled device (CCD), 26, 27
Characteristics of Image Operations, 44
Classification, 163
Clustering, 170
Clustering-based segmentation, 135, 150
CMY color model, 34
Color image, 6, 7, 21
Color Models, 34
Comparison of edge detection
    operators, 103
Counting Objects with OpenCV, 185

D

Dilation and Erosion, 151

E

Edge-based segmentation, 135, 150
Edge Detection, 73
Edge detection operators, 73
Edge Detection with OpenCV, 183
Edge localization, 77

Edge points detection, 77
Elements of Digital Image Processing
    System, 51

F

Factors influencing image noise., 63
frequency domain, 107
Frequency Domain Flow, 109

G

Gaussian High-Pass Filter, 123
Gaussian Low-Pass Filter, 115
GIF (Graphics Interchange Format), 48
Global operator, 44
Grayscale image, 5, 21, 30

H

Hexagonal sampling, 46
High-Pass Filters/Sharpening Filters,
    119
Histogram-based segmentation, 134, 142
Hit-or-Miss Transform, 159
How SVMs Work?, 165
HSV color model, 34, 36, 37
Hyperplane, 164

I

Ideal High-Pass Filter, 119
Ideal Low-Pass Filter, 110
Image Blurring, 180
Image Borders, 182
Image Conversion to Grayscale Format
    with OpenCV, 183
Image Formation, 24–26
Image Formats, 46
Image Noise, 61
Image processing, 1-8
Image Resizing, 179

Image Segmentation, 131
Image smoothing, 77
Impulse Noise, 65
Intensity, Brightness, and Contrast, 30

J

JPEG (Joint Photographic Experts
          Group), 47

K

k-Means Clustering, 170
k-Nearest Neighbor, 166
Krisch compass mask, 88

L

Laplacian operator, 100
Line edges/discontinuity, 75
Local operator, 44
Low-Pass Filters, 110
Low-Pass Filters versus High-Pass
          Filters, 127

M

MATLAB, 11
Morphological transforms-based
          segmentation, 135, 150

O

OpenCV, 11, 12
OpenCV Installation, 177

P

Photoelectronic Noise, 63
Photon Noise, 63
Pixel, 3, 4, 6, 23
Pixel Resolution and Pixel Density,
          31–33
PNG (Portable Network Graphic), 49
Point operation, 44
Predicting Forest Fire with OpenCV, 185

Prerequisites, 19
Prewitt operator, 83

Q

Quantization, 27, 29

R

Ramp edges/discontinuity, 75
RAW Format, 49
Rectangular sampling, 46
Region-based segmentation,
          135, 145
Region-Growing Method, 145
Region Split-and-Merge
          Technique, 147
Regression, 163
RGB, 8, 26, 27
RGB Color Model, 34
Robinson compass mask, 86
Roof edges/discontinuity, 75

S

Salt-and-Pepper Noise, 66
Sampling, 27, 29
Segmentation algorithm based on a
          global threshold, 136
Segmentation algorithm based
          on a variable
          threshold, 138
Segmentation algorithm based on
          multiple thresholds, 142
Selection of Global Threshold Using
          Otsu Method, 137
Sobel operator, 79
Spatial versus frequency
          domain, 108
Step edges/discontinuity, 75
Steps in Digital Image Processing, 49
Storage, 1, 2, 4, 6, 21, 29
Structured Noise, 67
Subtractive Color, 35
Support Vector Machine (SVM), 164
Support Vectors, 165

T

Texture-based segmentation
     approaches, 135
Thermal Noise, 64
Thresholding method, 134
TIFF (Tag Image File Format), 47
Tools for Image Processing, 11
Types of edges, 73
Types of image noise., 63
Types of Neighbourhoods, 45
Types of Segmentation, 134

W

What edges are?, 73, 74
Why detect edges?, 73, 74

Y

YUV color model, 34

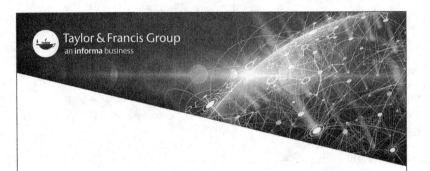

Printed in the United States
by Baker & Taylor Publisher Services